GRADE

4

# Word Analysis Workbook

**Pearson Education, Inc., 330 Hudson Street, New York, NY 10013**

ISBN-13: 978-0-328-96305-8
ISBN-10:   0-328-96305-4
4      18

# Contents

## Spelling

Name _____

# Short Vowels VCCV

**Classifying** Write the list word that fits each group.

1. rules, game, winner, _____
2. wheels, trunk, hood, _____
3. foot, toe, hand, _____
4. mistake, error, mishap, _____
5. cotton, wool, silk, _____
6. baseball, football, basketball, _____
7. pancake, road, dough, _____
8. otter, wolf, horse, _____
9. mean, plan, aim, _____
10. iron, attract, pole, _____
11. meeting, gathering, assembly, _____
12. habit, ritual, routine, _____
13. hat, scarf, earmuffs, _____

1. _____
2. _____
3. _____
4. _____
5. _____
6. _____
7. _____
8. _____
9. _____
10. _____
11. _____
12. _____
13. _____

**Context Clues** Choose a list word to complete each sentence of the script. Write the word.

14. Bowler 1: Hooray! I got a strike! Did you see it __?
15. Bowler 2: I __ your skill.
16. Bowler 3: The ball looked as if it had been shot from a __.
17. Bowler 1: My bowling __ is perfect!
18. Bowler 2: Then how come your ball just rolled into the __?
19. Bowler 1: All of a __ I just lost control of the ball.
20. Bowler 1: You __! I think you enjoyed my mistake.

14. _____
15. _____
16. _____
17. _____
18. _____
19. _____
20. _____

© Pearson Education, Inc., 4

**Home Activity** Your child spelled words with short vowels in VCCV pattern. Read the script aloud with your child. Have your child spell the list words with closed eyes.

1

Name _____

# Short Vowels VCCV

**Proofread a Newspaper Column** Circle five misspelled words in the newspaper column. Write the words correctly. Then write the sentence that has a punctuation mistake correctly.

1. _____  2. _____
3. _____  4. _____
5. _____  6. _____

**Proofread Words** Circle the correctly spelled word. Write the word.

| | | | | |
|---|---|---|---|---|
| 7. | cannon | cannen | kannon | 7. _____ |
| 8. | mignet | magnet | manget | 8. _____ |
| 9. | accident | ecident | eccident | 9. _____ |
| 10. | ingune | engine | ingine | 10. _____ |
| 11. | soccor | socor | soccer | 11. _____ |
| 12. | fabrik | fibrak | fabric | 12. _____ |

© Pearson Education, Inc., 4

**Home Activity** Your child identified misspelled words with short vowels in VCCV pattern. Say each spelling word. Ask your child to name the short vowel in the first syllable.

Name _____

# Long *a* and *i*

**Rhyme Time** Complete the rhymes with a list word from the box.

**Soccer Score**

The chances of scoring seemed (**1**)____.

Young Pee Wee lacked weight, strength, and (**2**)____.

He fell down with a (**3**)____.

The ball bounced off his (**4**)____,

And it soared through the goal on the (**5**)____.

1. _____
2. _____
3. _____
4. _____
5. _____

**Fishing Trip**

The fisherman left home at (**6**)____

And patiently set out with his (**7**)____.

But the fish just weren't bitin'.

Did the fisherman (**8**)____

Those fish that refused to be (**9**)____?

6. _____
7. _____
8. _____
9. _____

**Winter Drive**

As we drove down the icy (**10**)____

With our windshield covered with (**11**)____,

We started to (**12**)____

The idea of a (**13**)____.

It was slow going, to our (**14**)____.

10. _____
11. _____
12. _____
13. _____
14. _____

**Word Groups** Write the missing list word that belongs in each group.

**15.** ponytail, pigtails,

_____

**16.** wheat, rice,

_____

**17.** feature, characteristic,

_____

**18.** fig, date,

_____

**19.** aspect, fact,

_____

**20.** taut, close fitting,

_____

**Home Activity** Your child spelled words with *ai*, *eigh*, *ay*, and *igh*. Say a list word and ask your child to write it.

# Long *a* and *i*

**Proofread Directions** Read the following directions for making a wood puppet. Circle five misspelled words and write them correctly on the lines. Change the sentence fragments to a complete sentence and write the sentence.

Make sure you all ways work carefully with tools.
Measure wood for the hight you want.
Sand the wood in the direction of the grain.
Cut ate pieces for jointed arms and legs.
Spray on paint.
Braid some wool for hair.
Glue the hair on tite.
Add detale.
Make sure the puppet. Works
with right and left hands.

1. _____    2. _____
3. _____    4. _____
5. _____    6. _____
_____

**Finish the Sentences** Circle the underlined list word that is spelled correctly. Write the word.

7. The <u>freight</u> <u>frate</u> train has over 150 cars.                    7. _____
8. This kind of <u>raysin</u> <u>raisin</u> has no seeds.                       8. _____
9. The horses pulled the <u>sleigh</u> <u>slay</u>.                             9. _____
10. The <u>thy</u> <u>thigh</u> bone is the strongest bone in the body.       10. _____
11. Your answer is <u>rite</u> <u>right</u>.                                   11. _____
12. Generosity is a good <u>treight</u> <u>trait</u> to have.                  12. _____
13. "I forgot my homework," he said with <u>dismay</u> <u>dismeigh</u>.        13. _____
14. "Bring it in tomorrow," his teacher said with a <u>sy</u> <u>sigh</u>.     14. _____

© Pearson Education, Inc., 4

**School + Home**

**Home Activity** Your child identified misspelled words with *ai, eigh, ay,* and *igh*. Take turns quizzing each other on the spelling words.

Name _____

# Long e and o

| Spelling Words | | | | |
|---|---|---|---|---|
| sweet | each | three | least | freedom |
| below | throat | float | foam | flown |
| greet | season | croak | shallow | eagle |
| indeed | rainbow | grown | seaweed | hollow |

**Opposites** Write the list words that have the opposite or almost opposite meaning to the words below.

1. sour
2. most
3. sink
4. dismiss
5. newborn
6. solid
7. above
8. all
9. deep
10. limits

1. _____
2. _____
3. _____
4. _____
5. _____
6. _____
7. _____
8. _____
9. _____
10. _____

**Words in Context** Write a list word from the box to complete each sentence.

11. The ocean waves were white with ____.
12. Twins describe two people, and triplets describe ____ people.
13. Spring is my favorite ____.
14. When I was sick, I had a sore ____.
15. Some ocean plants are called ____.
16. When I lost my voice, I could only ____ like a frog.
17. The bald ____ is the national bird of the United States.
18. Spelling is serious business, ____.
19. I saw a ____ after the thunderstorm.
20. By the time I got the camera, the bird had ____ away.

11. _____
12. _____
13. _____
14. _____
15. _____
16. _____
17. _____
18. _____
19. _____
20. _____

**Home Activity** Your child wrote words with long e spelled *ee* or *ea* and long o spelled *oa* and *ow*. Say a word from the list and have your child write the word.

Name _____

# Long e and o

**Proofread a Menu** The restaurant owner is frantic! The new menus have errors that must be fixed before dinner tonight. Circle five misspelled words and write them correctly. Rewrite the sentence that has a capitalization error.

Seewead salad with vinegar and sesame seeds

Thre delight dish: shrimp, beef, and chicken

Hole crispy fried rainbow trout with lemon butter sauce

White hollo mushroom caps stuffed with crabmeat

Fresh vegetables in seeson

Chocolate cake with sweet whipped cream

Rootbeer float (vanilla or chocolate ice cream)

Coffee with hot milk foam

our Food is Organically grown.

1. _____   2. _____
3. _____   4. _____
5. _____   6. _____

**Proofread Words** Circle the correctly spelled word. Write the word

| 7. | leest | least | lest | 7. _____ |
| 8. | egle | eagle | eegle | 8. _____ |
| 9. | shallow | shalloe | shallo | 9. _____ |
| 10. | greet | grete | graet | 10. _____ |
| 11. | throte | throwt | throat | 11. _____ |
| 12. | floan | flown | flone | 12. _____ |
| 13. | beloa | below | belo | 13. _____ |
| 14. | freedowm | fredom | freedom | 14. _____ |
| 15. | indeed | indead | indede | 15. _____ |

**Home Activity** Your child identified misspelled words with *ee, ea, oa,* and *ow.* Ask your child to use each list word in a sentence.

Name _____

# Long e

| Spelling Words | | | | |
|---|---|---|---|---|
| prairie | calorie | honey | valley | money |
| finally | movie | country | empty | city |
| rookie | hockey | collie | breezy | jury |
| balcony | steady | alley | trolley | misty |

**Rhymes** Write the list word that rhymes with the underlined word.

1. Are you <u>ready</u>? Take it slow and ____.
2. Go to Main and First Streets, <u>Molly</u>. That's where you can catch the ____.
3. He paid a lot of <u>money</u> for the big jar of ____.
4. Let's make a <u>tally</u> of the number of cars in the ____.
5. Buffaloes are big and <u>hairy</u>. They used to roam across the ____.
6. "He's guilty!" the lawyer said with <u>fury</u> to the ____.
7. It was a <u>pity</u> he couldn't take a trip to the ____.
8. Sailing boats is <u>easy</u> when the wind is strong and ____.
9. "You're one smart <u>cookie</u>," said the coach to the ____.

1. _____
2. _____
3. _____
4. _____
5. _____
6. _____
7. _____
8. _____
9. _____

**Synonyms** Write the list word that means the same thing as the word or phrase.

10. raised porch
11. unit of energy
12. film
13. sheep dog
14. ice game
15. cash
16. vale
17. at last
18. nation
19. hazy
20. unfilled

10. _____
11. _____
12. _____
13. _____
14. _____
15. _____
16. _____
17. _____
18. _____
19. _____
20. _____

© Pearson Education, Inc., 4

**School + Home** **Home Activity** Your child wrote words that end with the long e sound spelled *ie*, *ey*, or *y*. Ask your child to say sentences using list words.

Name _____

# Long e

**Proofread an Ad** Jan wrote this ad to sell her dog. Circle five misspelled words. Write the words correctly. Then write the sentence that has a capitalization mistake correctly.

Dog for Sale

This colly is a honey of a dog! Very nice and steadey. Likes to play ball and hockie too. We're not asking a lot of monie for this fine Dog. He needs a good home because we are probablie moving to the city.

Call: 555-888-1234

1. _____  2. _____
3. _____  4. _____
5. _____
6. _____
_____

**Correct the Sentences** Cross out the misspelled list word in each sentence. Write the word correctly.

7. Please put the trash cans in the ally.          7. _____
8. It took the pioneers a long time to cross the prairy. 8. _____
9. Every spring, we put our potted plants on the balconie. 9. _____
10. The mistie fog made it hard to see the road.    10. _____
11. The long trip is finallee over.                 11. _____
12. The mailbox was emptie.                          12. _____
13. The rokie had a successful season.               13. _____
14. I like huney on my toast.                         14. _____
15. The moovy was funny.                              15. _____
16. I take the troley to the shops.                   16. _____

**School + Home** **Home Activity** Your child identified misspelled words that end with the long *e* sound spelled *ie, ey,* and *y.* Say a list word and spell it, stopping before the letter or letters that spell the long *e* sound at the end of the word. Have your child complete the word.

# Long *u*

| Spelling Words | | | | |
|---|---|---|---|---|
| usual | huge | flute | mood | smooth |
| threw | afternoon | scooter | juice | cruise |
| truth | bruise | cruel | excuse | pupil |
| groove | confuse | humor | duty | curfew |

**Antonyms** Write the list word that has the opposite or nearly
the opposite meaning as the word.

1. kind          1. _____
2. evening       2. _____
3. rough         3. _____
4. dishonesty    4. _____
5. caught        5. _____

**Synonyms** Write the list word that has the same or nearly
the same meaning as the word.

6. atmosphere    6. _____
7. instrument    7. _____
8. ridge         8. _____
9. sail          9. _____
10. forgive      10. _____

**Definitions** Write the list word that fits the definition.

11. _____ the time when children must be indoors
12. _____ a student
13. _____ discolored skin caused by an injury
14. _____ a riding toy with a platform, wheels, and a handlebar
15. _____ funny or amusing quality
16. _____ liquid taken from fruit or vegetables
17. _____ enormous
18. _____ a task a person is required to do
19. _____ ordinary
20. _____ perplex, mix up

**Home Activity** Your child wrote words with long *u* sounds spelled *u-consonant-e, ew, oo, ui,* and *u*.
Say a list word and have your child write it.

# Long *u*

**Proofread a Script** Read the script that a DJ will read on the radio. Circle six spelling errors and write the words correctly. Add quotation marks where they are needed.

**DJ:** Good afternune, listeners. Today, we're taking a crewse down memory lane. I'm going to play some smoothe sounds from the past. But first, here's a word from our sponsor.

**Commercial Spot:** Is it breakfast as usual? How about a huge energy boost? Drink some OranGee orange juce today. Don't confuse it with other breakfast drinks!

**DJ:** Now, it's time for the news! A high schewl pupil suffered a huge bruze when he fell off his scooter. I have no clue what happened, said the student.

1. _____
2. _____
3. _____
4. _____
5. _____
6. _____

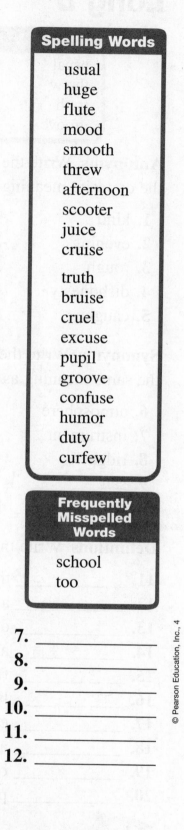

**Spelling Words**

usual
huge
flute
mood
smooth
threw
afternoon
scooter
juice
cruise
truth
bruise
cruel
excuse
pupil
groove
confuse
humor
duty
curfew

**Frequently Misspelled Words**

school
too

**Proofread Words** Circle the word that is spelled correctly. Write the word.

7. Abby likes to read stories that have some **humor  hewmor**.
8. The captain **thrue  threw** a life jacket to each passenger.
9. "There is no **excus  excuse** for this mess," said Mom.
10. It's always a good idea to tell the **truth  trueth**.
11. "Don't stay out past **curfoo  curfew**," Dad warned.
12. The **huge  hug** truck rattled the windows as it passed our house.

7. _____
8. _____
9. _____
10. _____
11. _____
12. _____

© Pearson Education, Inc., 4

**Home Activity** Your child identified misspelled words with *u-consonant-e*, *ew*, *oo*, *ui*, and *u*. Ask your child to use list words to make up a radio announcement or commercial.

# Short Vowels VCCV

| Spelling Words | | | | |
|---|---|---|---|---|
| admire | magnet | contest | method | custom |
| rally | soccer | engine | sudden | finger |
| accident | mitten | intend | fabric | flatten |
| rascal | gutter | mammal | happen | cannon |

**Synonyms** Write the list word that is a synonym for each word.

**1.** quick _____

**2.** occur _____

**3.** scoundrel _____

**4.** squash _____

**5.** cloth _____

**6.** respect _____

**7.** habit _____

**8.** competition _____

**9.** plan _____

**10.** technique _____

**Definitions** Write the list word beside its definition.

**11.** object that attracts iron _____

**12.** unlucky event that harms _____

**13.** a large gun on a fixed base _____

**14.** a sport played by kicking a round ball _____

**15.** animal that produces milk for its young _____

**16.** to come together _____

**17.** a roadside channel _____

**18.** a part of the hand _____

**19.** a machine that uses energy _____

**20.** a kind of glove _____

**Home Activity** Your child spelled words with the short vowel pattern VCCV. Have your child point out list words with short vowel *a* in the first syllable. Repeat for each vowel.

# Long *a* and *i*

| Spelling Words | | | | |
|---|---|---|---|---|
| sigh | right | weigh | eight | detail |
| height | spray | braid | bait | grain |
| slight | thigh | tight | raisin | trait |
| highway | frighten | dismay | freight | sleigh |

**Classifying** Write the list word that fits each group.

1. arm, neck, hand, _____
2. laugh, cry, yawn, _____
3. pole, line, hook, _____
4. one, five, twelve, _____
5. avenue, street, lane, _____
6. length, width, depth, _____
7. prune, apricot, cherry, _____
8. scare, startle, spook, _____
9. wash, dry, comb, _____
10. skis, snow fort, sled, _____

1. _____
2. _____
3. _____
4. _____
5. _____
6. _____
7. _____
8. _____
9. _____
10. _____

**Alphabetize** Read the words. Write the list word from the box that comes between them in a dictionary.

11. freezer _____ French
12. go _____ group
13. slam _____ sloop
14. tomb _____ trip
15. dish _____ displace
16. tiara _____ time
17. week _____ window
18. sport _____ spring
19. depot _____ develop
20. reserve _____ ring

| right |
| --- |
| detail |
| grain |
| slight |
| dismay |
| spray |
| freight |
| tight |
| weigh |
| trait |

*© Pearson Education, Inc., 4*

**Home Activity** Your child spelled words with long *a* and *i* spelled *ai*, *eigh*, *ay*, and *igh*. Ask your child to name all the ways he or she can spell long *a* and long *i* and write an example word for each spelling.

# Long e and o

**Name** _____

| Spelling Words | | | | |
|---|---|---|---|---|
| sweet | each | three | least | freedom |
| below | throat | float | foam | flown |
| greet | season | croak | shallow | eagle |
| indeed | rainbow | grown | seaweed | hollow |

**Word Patterns** Fill in the missing letters to write a list word.

1. S H __ L __ O __
2. __ A __ N B O __
3. __ __ E E __ __ M
4. __ E A S __ __
5. S __ __ W __ __ D
6. __ __ R O __ __
7. __ O L __ __ W
8. __ N __ E E __
9. __ __ C H
10. __ L __ T
11. G __ O W __

**Crossword Puzzle** Use the clues below
to solve the puzzle.

**Across**
2. welcome
4. many white bubbles
5. opposite of *above*
7. opposite of *sour*

**Down**
1. frog sound
3. large, powerful bird
4. fly, flew, _____
6. opposite of *most*

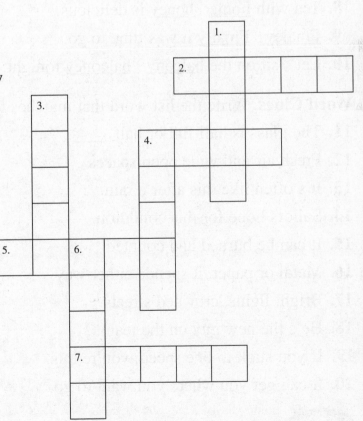

**Home Activity** Your child spelled words with long *e* and *o* spelled *ee*, *ea*, *oa*, and *ow*. Read each list
word. Have your child tell the spelling of the long vowel sound in the word.

13

# Long e

**Finish the Sentences** Circle the underlined list word that is spelled correctly. Write the word.

1. My favorite dog is the border <u>colley</u>   <u>collie</u>.

2. Sam and I went to a <u>hockey</u>   <u>hockie</u> game.

3. The kitten ran into the <u>ally</u>   <u>alley</u>.

4. The <u>jurie</u>   <u>jury</u> listened carefully to the lawyer.

5. Crops in the <u>vally</u>   <u>valley</u> were green and healthy.

6. That <u>movie</u>   <u>movey</u> about sailors was exciting.

7. Some <u>praire</u>   <u>prairie</u> grasses grow ten feet tall.

8. Tea with <u>honie</u>   <u>honey</u> is delicious.

9. <u>Finaley</u>   <u>Finally</u> it was time to go.

10. Let's sit on the <u>balcony</u>   <u>balconey</u> tonight.

1. _____
2. _____
3. _____
4. _____
5. _____
6. _____
7. _____
8. _____
9. _____
10. _____

**Word Clues** Write the list word that matches the clue.

11. The glass is half full or half _____.

12. Fresh air and wide open spaces

13. It's often like this after a rain.

14. Sailors hope for this condition.

15. It can be burned and counted.

16. Metal or paper, it spends either way.

17. Bright lights, crowded streets

18. He's the new guy on the team.

19. If you stick to one speed, you're this.

20. It can get you where you want to go.

11. _____
12. _____
13. _____
14. _____
15. _____
16. _____
17. _____
18. _____
19. _____
20. _____

© Pearson Education, Inc., 4

**School + Home**

**Home Activity** Your child used words with the long *e* sound spelled *ie*, *ey*, and *y*. Say each list word and spell it incorrectly. Have your child tell you the correct spelling.

Name _____

# Long *u*

| Spelling Words | | | | |
|---|---|---|---|---|
| usual | huge | flute | mood | smooth |
| threw | afternoon | scooter | juice | cruise |
| truth | bruise | cruel | excuse | pupil |
| groove | confuse | humor | duty | curfew |

**Words in Context** Write a list word from the box to complete each sentence.

1. When I fell, I got a _____ on my knee.

2. Hap moved quickly through traffic on his ____.

3. The pitcher _____ the ball 95 miles per hour.

4. Julie played a solo on her _____.

5. Salsa music puts me in a good _____.

6. Most people like _____ with their breakfast.

7. A comic needs a good sense of _____.

8. Bad directions might _____ you.

9. I usually get sleepy in the middle of the _____.

10. A horse is large, but an elephant is _____.

1. _____

2. _____

3. _____

4. _____

5. _____

6. _____

7. _____

8. _____

9. _____

10. _____

**Word Scramble** Unscramble the list words and write the letters on the lines.

11. suula        _____

12. frecuw       _____

13. clure        _____

14. sceuxe       _____

15. goover       _____

16. scrieu       _____

17. uhttr        _____

18. tudy         _____

19. lippu        _____

20. mthoso       _____

© Pearson Education, Inc., 4

**Home Activity** Your child used words with long *u* spelled *u*-consonant-*e*, *ew*, *oo*, *ui*, and *u*. Say each list word and have your child spell it. Then have him or her use it in a sentence.

# Adding -s and -es

| Spelling Words | | | | |
|---|---|---|---|---|
| monkeys | friends | plays | supplies | taxes |
| holidays | months | companies | costumes | sandwiches |
| hobbies | daisies | delays | scratches | counties |
| teammates | memories | bunches | batteries | donkeys |

**Multiple Meanings** Some words can be either a noun (name of a person, place, or thing) or a verb (word that shows action). Write the list word that begins with the given letter and can be used to complete both sentences.

1. The traffic **d**_____ made everyone late.
   When the bus breaks down, it **d**_____ our arrival.

1. _____

2. The cat **s**_____ the rug to sharpen its claws.
   I got these **s**_____ when I fell off my bike.

2. _____

3. The government adds **t**_____ to most things we buy.
   Running marathons **t**_____ my energy.

3. _____

4. The army **s**_____ troops with food, clothing, and shelter.
   Have you bought everything on your list of school **s**_____?

4. _____

5. *Romeo and Juliet* and *Hamlet* are **p**___ by Shakespeare.
   The harpist **p**_____ soft music at weddings.

5. _____

6. It gets crowded when everyone **b**_____ up by the door.
   Ten **b**_____ of grapes were passed out to the team.

6. _____

**Adding -s or -es** Add -s or -es to make each word plural. Write the word.

7. monkey _____

8. holiday _____

9. costume _____

10. battery _____

11. sandwich _____

12. company _____

13. county _____

14. daisy _____

15. donkey _____

16. friend _____

17. hobby _____

18. memory _____

19. teammate _____

20. month _____

**Home Activity** Your child spelled words that end with -s or -es. Say the singular form of the list word and have your child say and spell its plural form.

16

© Pearson Education, Inc., 4

Name _____

# Adding -s and -es

**Proofread a Dialogue** Read the dialogue and circle five spelling mistakes. Then write the words correctly. Cross out the punctuation error and write the sentence correctly.

Spelling Words

monkeys
friends
plays
supplies
taxes
holidays
months
companies
costumes
sandwiches

hobbies
daisies
delays
scratches
counties
teammates
memories
bunches
batteries
donkeys

> **Rick:** Which plays are you trying out for.
>
> **Hal:** I want to be in the one about six silly monkeyes.
>
> **Kim:** I'm sure the costumees are itchy.
>
> **Hal:** You're right! All that furry stuff probably scratches alot.
>
> **Kim:** Ami, one of my friends, wants to try out, too. Acting is one of her hobbys.
>
> **Rick:** Well, I hope we all have good memores.

1. _____   2. _____

3. _____   4. _____

5. _____

6. _____

**Proofread Words** Circle the correctly spelled word. Write the word.

Frequently Misspelled Words

a lot
because

| | | | | |
|---|---|---|---|---|
| 7. taxs | taxse | taxes | 7. _____ |
| 8. countys | counties | counteys | 8. _____ |
| 9. months | monthes | monthies | 9. _____ |
| 10. batterys | batteryes | batteries | 10. _____ |
| 11. teamates | teammates | teammats | 11. _____ |
| 12. supplies | supplys | supplyes | 12. _____ |
| 13. frinds | frends | friends | 13. _____ |
| 14. scratches | skratches | scrathes | 14. _____ |
| 15. daysies | daisies | dasies | 15. _____ |

**Home Activity** Your child identified misspelled words with -s and -es endings. Ask your child to use the words in Exercises 7–15 in sentences.

# Irregular Plurals

| Spelling Words | | | | |
|---|---|---|---|---|
| videos | feet | potatoes | themselves | lives |
| leaves | cliffs | men | halves | moose |
| radios | sheep | cuffs | beliefs | patios |
| children | tornadoes | tomatoes | hoofs | loaves |

**Words in Context** Write a list word to complete the sentence.

1. When the siren sounded, people turned on their ____.      1. _____
2. The weather report warned that ____ were on the way.      2. _____
3. Then the ____ on the trees began to sway.                 3. _____
4. The wind could lift a person off his or her ____.         4. _____
5. Even grown ____ and women feared the powerful storm.      5. _____
6. After the storm, people walked out onto their ____.       6. _____
7. They wanted to see the damage for ____.                   7. _____
8. The tornado had divided the town into two ____.           8. _____
9. In one half, the houses were stacked up like ____ of bread.  9. _____
10. In the other half, even ____ on their vines had not been disturbed.  10. _____
11. The neighbors pushed up their ____ and went to work.     11. _____
12. Everyone was grateful that no ____ had been lost.        12. _____

**Definitions** Write the list word that matches the definition.

13. values and ideals                     13. _____
14. young people                          14. _____
15. steep rocks                           15. _____
16. pictures on monitors                  16. _____
17. large members of the deer family      17. _____
18. starchy foods with dark skins         18. _____
19. horses' feet                          19. _____
20. wooly animals                         20. _____

**Home Activity** Your child wrote irregular plural words. Say the singular form of each spelling word. Ask your child to say and spell the plural form.

# Irregular Plurals

**Proofread an E-mail** The computer's spelling and grammar check isn't working. Circle five misspelled words. Add the missing period.

Spelling Words

videos
feet
potatoes
themselves
lives
leaves
cliffs
men
halves
moose

radios
sheep
cuffs
beliefs
patios
children
tornadoes
tomatoes
hoofs
loaves

Dear CityPal95,

Today I went to herd sheep with my cousin. Later, we dug up some potatoes  In the afternoon, we climbed the cliffes by the river. When we got to the top, we saw some mooses. They shook their antlers and stamped their hoofs. Then thay ran away.

Tomorrow we're going to a picking party. That's when everyone gets together to play guitars and fiddles. All the childrens will dance and sing.

Have you seen any good videoes lately?

Later,
CountryMouse96

1. _____     2. _____
3. _____     4. _____
5. _____

Frequently Misspelled Words

they
went
said

**Proofread Words** Circle the plural word that is spelled correctly. Write it on the line.

| | | | | |
|---|---|---|---|---|
| 6. leaf | leafs | leaves | 6. | _____ |
| 7. feet | foots | foot | 7. | _____ |
| 8. radioes | radios | radis | 8. | _____ |
| 9. loafs | loaves | loafes | 9. | _____ |
| 10. potatos | potates | potatoes | 10. | _____ |
| 11. themselves | themselfs | themselfes | 11. | _____ |
| 12. cufes | cuffs | cuffes | 12. | _____ |

© Pearson Education, Inc., 4

**Home Activity** Your child identified misspelled irregular plural words. Say each spelling word. Ask your child to explain how the plural was formed.

Name _____

# Words with *ar, or*

**Missing Words** Write a list word to finish each chapter title. Use capital letters.

**Household Ecology**

Chapter 1: Make Nature Your **(1)**____

Chapter 2: Grow a Healthy **(2)**____

Chapter 3: Birds as **(3)**____ Visitors

Chapter 4: Turn Kitchen **(4)**____ into Gold

Chapter 5: Your Own Woody **(5)**____

**Stories from the South**

Chapter 1: "The **(6)**____ Traveler"

Chapter 2: "**(7)**____ Swamps"

Chapter 3: "Early **(8)**____ Fishing in the Carolinas"

**Your New Apartment**

Chapter 1: House or **(9)**____?

Chapter 2: How NOT to **(10)**____ with Your Landlord

1. _____

2. _____

3. _____

4. _____

5. _____

6. _____

7. _____

8. _____

9. _____

10. _____

**Multiple Meanings** Read the definitions. Write the list word that fits both meanings.

11. _____ a shape or to make

12. _____ sudden fear or a warning device

13. _____ the place where two walls come together or to trap

14. _____ to begin or to jump in surprise or fright

15. _____ one floor of a building or a tale

16. _____ strong wind with heavy rain or snow or to show anger

17. _____ a game or contest or to wear

18. _____ ahead or bold

19. _____ having a thin, cutting edge or smart

20. _____ active power or to make someone act against his or her will

**Home Activity** Your child wrote words with *ar* and *or*. Spell a list word. Ask your child to say the word and then use it in a sentence.

© Pearson Education, Inc., 4

Name _____

# Words with *ar, or*

**Proofread a Travel Brochure** Check the brochure before it goes to the printer. Circle six misspelled words. Write the words correctly. Then correct the sentence fragment.

**Spelling Words**

All aboard! Daily sightseeing trains leave Tallahassee at six o'clock in the morening. Start your day right. With some delicious Flarida orange juice. Enjoy the view from the top storry of our observation car. Have lunch in everyone's favarit tearoom in Theodore, Alabama, and tour the graden. There's just time to hike in the forest around the Buffalo River before our last stop at Little Rock, Arkansaw.

**Spelling Words**

morning
forest
garbage
form
alarm
corner
story
argue
backyard
start

partner
storm
Florida
apartment
sport
force
forward
sharp
garden
Arkansas

1. _____    2. _____
3. _____    4. _____
5. _____    6. _____
7. _____
_____

**Missing Letters** Chose *ar* or *or* to complete each word. Then write the word.

8. _ _gue              8. _____
9. ap _ _ tment        9. _____
10. sh _ _ p           10. _____
11. p _ _ tner         11. _____
12. g _ _bage          12. _____
13. f _ _ ward         13. _____
14. sp _ _ t           14. _____
15. st _ _ m           15. _____
16. f _ _ ce           16. _____
17. g _ _ den          17. _____
18. al _ _ m           18. _____

**Frequently Misspelled Words**

favorite
morning

© Pearson Education, Inc., 4

**School + Home**

**Home Activity** Your child identified misspelled words with *ar* or *or*. Say list words and spell them incorrectly. Have your child correct your mistakes.

21

Name _____

# Consonant Pairs *ng, nk, ph, wh*

### Spelling Words

| | | | | |
|---|---|---|---|---|
| Thanksgiving | among | think | blank | graph |
| young | wheel | nephew | belong | whiskers |
| whisper | elephant | white | shrink | wharf |
| trunk | strong | blink | chunk | skunk |

**Context Clues** Write a list word to complete each saying.

1. The ____ never forgets.
2. The squeaky ____ gets the oil.
3. He vanished in the ____ of an eye.
4. Its fleece was ____ as snow.
5. The wet dog was as smelly as a ____.
6. I ____ therefore I am.
7. The weightlifter is as ____ as an ox.
8. I ate until I felt as stuffed as a ____ turkey.

1. _____
2. _____
3. _____
4. _____
5. _____
6. _____
7. _____
8. _____

**Classifying** Write the list word that fits into each group.

9. shout, talk, ____
10. between, in, ____
11. empty, unused, ____
12. childlike, immature, ____
13. chart, map, ____
14. reduce, decrease, ____
15. briefcase, suitcase, ____
16. piece, slab, ____
17. uncle, grandfather, ____
18. join, fit, ____
19. pier, dock, ____
20. beard, mustache, ____

9. _____
10. _____
11. _____
12. _____
13. _____
14. _____
15. _____
16. _____
17. _____
18. _____
19. _____
20. _____

© Pearson Education, Inc., 4

**Home Activity** Your child spelled words with *ng, nk, ph,* and *wh.* Say a list word and have your child spell the word and use it in a sentence.

Name _____

# Consonant Pairs *ng, nk, ph, wh*

**Proofread a Poster** Andy made a poster for the team fundraiser. Circle six words that are spelled incorrectly. Write the words correctly. Find the run-on sentence. Write it correctly.

> Come to the white elefant sale!
>
> Wen: Friday after Thanksgivin
>
> Where: Kennedy School Gym
>
> Why: To buy sports equipment for youg boys' and girls' sports teams
>
> One person's junk is another person's treasure, so bring a chunk of change to spend. Your children, nieces, and nefews will benefit. Everyone is welcome!
>
> We need some stronge people to help with setup come early.

| | |
|---|---|
| 1. _____ | 2. _____ |
| 3. _____ | 4. _____ |
| 5. _____ | 6. _____ |
| 7. _____ |

**Spelling Words**

Thanksgiving
among
think
blank
graph
young
wheel
nephew
belong
whiskers

whisper
elephant
white
shrink
wharf
trunk
strong
blink
chunk
skunk

**Frequently Misspelled Words**

where
when

**Proofread Words** Write the underlined words correctly. Then follow the directions. What you see may surprise you.

8. Draw a large red dot in the middle of a sheet of <u>graf</u> paper.　　8. _____

9. Stare at the dot for 30 seconds. Don't <u>blin</u>!　　9. _____

10. Then stare at a <u>blanc</u> wall for 15 seconds.　　10. _____

11. A <u>wite</u> wall works best.　　11. _____

12. What color dot do you <u>thik</u> you will see?　　12. _____

**Home Activity** Your child identified misspelled words with *ng, nk, ph,* or *wh*. Ask your child to spell the words he or she did not write when answering the questions on this page.

Name _____

# Words with *ear, ir, our, ur*

| Spelling Words | | | | |
|---|---|---|---|---|
| return | courage | surface | purpose | first |
| turkey | heard | early | turtle | birthday |
| journal | courtesy | nourish | purse | furniture |
| search | curtain | burrow | hamburger | survey |

**Missing Words** Write two list words to complete each sentence correctly.

Baby Teddy is having his **(1)**____ **(2)**____ party today.

1. _____  2. _____

We bought new **(3)**____ for my bedroom and a new **(4)**____ for the window.

3. _____  4. _____

It takes **(5)**____ for a box **(6)**____ to cross a road.

5. _____  6. _____

Mom had to **(7)**____ through her **(8)**____ to find a tissue.

7. _____  8. _____

The **(9)**____ of **(10)**____ is to put others at ease.

9. _____  10. _____

Like other birds, the **(11)**____ wakes **(12)**____.

11. _____  12. _____

**Analogies** Write list words to complete each analogy.

13. *Bread* is to *sandwich* as *bun* is to ____.       13. _____
14. *Blanket* is to *warm* as *food* is to ____.        14. _____
15. *Eye* is to *saw* as *ear* is to ____.              15. _____
16. *Go* is to *come* as *leave* is to ____.            16. _____
17. *Read* is to *novel* as *write* is to ____.         17. _____
18. *Draw* is to *map* as *measure* is to ____.         18. _____
19. *Down* is to *dive* as *up* is to ____.             19. _____
20. *Bird* is to *nest* as *rabbit* is to ____.         20. _____

**Home Activity** Your child spelled words with *ear, ir, our,* and *ur*. Say a list word and have your child spell the word and use it in a sentence.

24

Name _____

# Words with *ear, ir, our, ur*

**Proofread a Journal Entry** Samantha made mistakes as she wrote her journal entry. Circle six misspelled words and write them correctly. Insert quotation marks where they are needed.

Today was my birthday! I was up very erly. Usually I run right down to breakfast, but today I was as slow as a tertle. As I walked into the kitchen, I herd my family yell, Surprise!

My family gave me a new purse and this brand new jurnal! My friends took me out for a hambirger at lunch. For dinner, we had my favorite—turkey! The only present I have to retearn is a shirt that is too small.

I'll write more tomorrow,
Samantha

1. _____   2. _____
3. _____   4. _____
5. _____   6. _____

**Proofread Words** Circle the word that is spelled correctly. Write it on the line.

| | | | |
|---|---|---|---|
| 7. courage | corage | curage | 7. _____ |
| 8. searface | sirface | surface | 8. _____ |
| 9. curtesy | cirtesy | courtesy | 9. _____ |
| 10. survey | sourvey | sirvey | 10. _____ |
| 11. bourrow | birrow | burrow | 11. _____ |
| 12. curtain | courtain | curtin | 12. _____ |
| 13. perse | purse | pirse | 13. _____ |
| 14. pirpose | purpase | purpose | 14. _____ |

**School + Home**

**Home Activity** Your child identified misspelled words with *ear, ir, our,* and *ur*. Ask your child to write *courtesy* and make up a journal entry about a time he or she was courteous.

25

Name _____

# Adding -*s* and -*es*

| Spelling Words | | | | |
|---|---|---|---|---|
| monkeys | friends | plays | supplies | taxes |
| holidays | months | companies | costumes | sandwiches |
| hobbies | daisies | delays | scratches | counties |
| teammates | memories | bunches | batteries | donkeys |

**Naming Classes** Write the list word that describes each group.

1. Fourth of July, Thanksgiving, Labor Day
2. hiking, collecting stamps, reading
3. flower shop, bank, grocery store
4. AA, AAA, D, 9-volt
5. July, February, October
6. ham and cheese, hamburger, peanut butter
7. pencils, paper, ruler, markers
8. howler, capuchin, marmoset
9. bananas, grapes, bouquets of flowers
10. pitcher, catcher, shortstop

**Word Meanings** Write the list word beside the phrase that means the same.

11. people who know and like you
12. dramas acted on the stage
13. money paid to a government
14. actors' clothing
15. long-eared relatives of the horse
16. things remembered
17. flowers with white or pink petals
18. areas into which a state is divided
19. marks or cuts made by sharp objects
20. makes late by slowing or stopping

© Pearson Education, Inc., 4

**Home Activity** Your child learned to spell the plural forms of words by adding -*s* or -*es*. Write the singular form of each word and have your child tell if and how it changes to form the plural.

Name _____

# Irregular Plurals

**Context Clues** Choose a list word to complete each sentence. Write the word.

1. A strong wind blew the _____ off of trees.  _____
2. The weather service sent out a warning for _____.  _____
3. People sat in basements and listened to _____.  _____
4. _____ and their parents waited patiently.  _____
5. The furniture on _____ had to be put away.  _____
6. Most people thought _____ lucky.  _____
7. Going to the basement was a safety tip that saved many _____.  _____
8. Over a meal of meat and _____, people smiled.  _____
9. They rolled up the _____ of their sleeves and went to work.  _____

**Word Clues** Write the list word that answers the clue.

10. Your socks are filled with these.  _____
11. We get wool from them.  _____
12. A baker makes these.  _____
13. A tasty red food with *toes* in them.  _____
14. You watch these after an event happens.  _____

**Watch the Ending** Circle the correctly spelled list word.

15. patios        patioes
16. hoofs         hoofes
17. cliffs        clives
18. halfs         halves
19. loafs         loaves
20. beliefs       believs

© Pearson Education, Inc., 4

**Home Activity** Your child learned irregular plural words. Have your child make flash cards with the singular form of each list word on one side and the plural form on the other. Use the cards to quiz each other.

# Words with *ar, or*

| Spelling Words | | | | |
|---|---|---|---|---|
| morning | forest | garbage | form | alarm |
| corner | story | argue | backyard | start |
| partner | storm | Florida | apartment | sport |
| force | forward | sharp | garden | Arkansas |

**Tried and True Sayings** Write the list word that correctly completes each saying.

1. Happiness begins right in your own _____.

2. He is as _____ as a tack.

3. She can't see the _____ for the trees.

4. Sleep. Things will look better in the _____.

5. After a _____, a rainbow comes.

6. For every step _____, I take two steps back.

7. Let's begin again to make a fresh _____.

8. _____, the Natural State!

9. _____, it's the Sunshine State!

10. Thanks for being such a good _____.

**Word Meanings** Write the list word that fits each definition.

11. things thrown away

12. a home in a larger building

13. something's shape

14. angle where two walls meet

15. sudden feeling of fear

16. to disagree

17. power or strength

18. co-worker or associate

19. a tale of an event

20. a plot for growing vegetables

© Pearson Education, Inc., 4

**Home Activity** Your child learned to distinguish words with *ar* and *or*. Have your child write list words and highlight *ar* and *or* in contrasting colors.

Name _____

# Consonant Pairs *ng, nk, ph, wh*

| Spelling Words | | | | |
| --- | --- | --- | --- | --- |
| Thanksgiving | among | think | blank | graph |
| young | wheel | nephew | belong | whiskers |
| whisper | elephant | white | shrink | wharf |
| trunk | strong | blink | chunk | skunk |

**Antonyms** Write the list word that has the opposite, or nearly the opposite, meaning as the word.

1. old      _____
2. shout      _____
3. weak      _____
4. black      _____
5. grow      _____

**Synonyms** Write the list word that has the same, or nearly the same, meaning as the word.

6. beard      _____
7. box      _____
8. ponder      _____
9. dock      _____
10. with      _____

**Words in Context** Write a list word from the box to complete each sentence.

11. Carl cut himself a large _____ of cheese.      _____
12. The _____ uses a bad smell to keep predators away.      _____
13. We eat a huge meal on _____ Day.      _____
14. The wagon has a loose _____.      _____
15. The zoo has monkeys and an _____.      _____
16. Zach is my brother's son, or my _____.      _____
17. The bright light made me _____ my eyes.      _____
18. Write your answer on the _____ line.      _____
19. Those marbles _____ to me; they are mine.      _____
20. I made a _____ showing how I have grown.      _____

© Pearson Education, Inc., 4

 **Home Activity** Your child learned words with consonant pairs *ng, nk, ph,* and *wh.* Have your child identify the consonant pair in each list word. Then help your child think of other words with these spellings.

Name _____

# Words with *ear, ir, our, ur*

## Spelling Words

| | | | | |
|---|---|---|---|---|
| return | courage | surface | purpose | first |
| turkey | heard | early | turtle | birthday |
| journal | courtesy | nourish | purse | furniture |
| search | curtain | burrow | hamburger | survey |

**Classifying** Write the list word that fits each group.

1. chicken, pheasant, quail, _____               _____

2. desks, tables, beds, sofas, _____        _____

3. bedspread, screen, tablecloth, _____    _____

4. measure, examine, map out, _____     _____

5. lizard, snake, alligator, _____           _____

6. nest, cave, den, _____                  _____

7. book, magazine, newspaper, _____     _____

8. hot dog, chicken salad, barbecue, _____   _____

9. bag, briefcase, pouch, _____         _____

10. fourth, third, second, _____         _____

**Word Scramble** Unscramble each list word and write it on the line.

11. thradiby    _____

12. nuterr    _____

13. sharce    _____

14. greacuo    _____

15. radeh    _____

16. restucoy    _____

17. furcesa    _____

18. raley    _____

19. hournis    _____

20. ropesup    _____

**Home Activity** Your child learned words spelled with *ear, ir, our,* and *ur*. Say each list word. Have your child explain the word's meaning and spell it aloud.

© Pearson Education, Inc., 4

# Adding -ed and -ing

## Spelling Words

| | | | | |
|---|---|---|---|---|
| watched | watching | danced | dancing | studied |
| studying | stopped | stopping | dried | drying |
| happened | happening | noticed | noticing | robbed |
| robbing | slipped | slipping | hurried | hurrying |

**Definitons** Write a list word to fit each definition. If the verb in the definition ends with -ed, write an -ed word. If the verb ends with -ing, write an -ing word.

**1.** raced

_____

**2.** paying attention

_____

**3.** occurring

_____

**4.** reviewed for a test

_____

**5.** ended

_____

**6.** falling on ice

_____

**7.** moved to music

_____

**8.** observed

_____

**9.** stealing

_____

**10.** dehydrated

_____

**Complete the Sentence** Read the base word at the beginning of each sentence. Write the correct form of the base word to complete the sentence.

**11. hurry** Did you see anyone ____ by here lately?

**11.** _____

**12. happen** No I didn't. What ____?

**12.** _____

**13. stop** Well, I heard cars ____ quickly.

**13.** _____

**14. dance** People seemed to be ____ around in front of the bank.

**14.** _____

**15. rob** Then I realized they were shouting that the bank had been ____.

**15.** _____

**16. notice** Soon I ____ the sound of sirens.

**16.** _____

**17. study** I saw police ____ the crime scene.

**17.** _____

**18. slip** The thief had ____ away.

**18.** _____

**19. watch** Now the police are ____ the bank's videotape.

**19.** _____

**20. dry** Soon the criminal will be ____ his tears in jail.

**20.** _____

**Home Activity** Your child wrote words with -ed and -ing endings. Say a list word and have your child spell the list word aloud.

31

Name _____

# Adding -ed and -ing

**Proofread a Story** Read the story. Circle six misspelled words and write them correctly. Rewrite the sentence that has a punctuation error.

**A Dancer Dreams**

After Katrina put on her costume, she stoped to look into the mirror.

"Maybe tonight I'll be notised, she said softly.

Katrina had been studing dancing for most of her fourteen years. She wacht other dancers become famous. Katrina hoped that would happen to her soon.

She struck her most graceful pose in front of the mirror. Then she openned the door and hurryed out to the stage.

1. _____
2. _____
3. _____
4. _____
5. _____
6. _____
7. _____

**Spelling Words**

watched
watching
danced
dancing
studied
studying
stopped
stopping
dried
drying

happened
happening
noticed
noticing
robbed
robbing
slipped
slipping
hurried
hurrying

**Frequently Misspelled Words**

swimming
stopped
happened
slipped
opened

**Proofread Words** Write the misspelled list word correctly.

8. driing _____
9. happing _____
10. sliped _____
11. danceed _____
12. robed _____
13. hurryng _____
14. noticeing _____
15. studyed _____
16. stoping _____
17. hapened _____
18. robing _____
19. dryed _____

© Pearson Education, Inc., 4

**Home Activity** Your child identified misspelled words with *-ed* and *-ing* endings. Say a base word, and have your child add the endings and spell the list words.

Name _____

# Homophones

| Spelling Words | | | | |
|---|---|---|---|---|
| two | to | too | piece | peace |
| break | brake | there | their | they're |
| threw | through | by | bye | beat |
| beet | thrown | throne | aloud | allowed |

**Word Meanings** Write the list word that has the same or almost the
same meaning as each word or phrase.

1. part
2. stop
3. finished
4. so long
5. rhythm
6. king's chair
7. spoken
8. they are
9. also
10. belonging to them

1. _____
2. _____
3. _____
4. _____
5. _____
6. _____
7. _____
8. _____
9. _____
10. _____

**Missing Words** Write a list word to complete each sentence.

11. Three is one more than ____.
12. The pitcher ____ the ball to first base.
13. I was afraid I had ____ my homework in the wastebasket.
14. Mom asked for some ____ and quiet.
15. Jon's face turns as red as a ____ when he blushes.
16. We aren't ____ to stay out after dark.
17. This book was written ____ my favorite author.
18. My brother is over ____ beside the car.
19. Sarah read her poem ____ the class.
20. You can take a ____ after you finish your chores.

11. _____
12. _____
13. _____
14. _____
15. _____
16. _____
17. _____
18. _____
19. _____
20. _____

**Home Activity** Your child wrote homophones. Use a list word in a sentence and have your child write
the word.

Name _____

# Homophones

**Proofread a Play**  Circle six spelling errors in the play. Write the words correctly on the lines. Find a sentence with a capitalization error and write it correctly.

**Mr. Dario:** A ball just went threw your window!

**Mr. Chala:** Did the window break?

**Mr. Dario:** Yes, I think a small peace cracked.

**Mr. Chala:** It's those neighbors playing they're game again!

**Mr. Dario:** I thought they weren't aloud to play by the house.

**Mr. Chala:** Soon Jim will be knocking on the door red as a beat.

**Mr. Dario:** well, children need to play too.

**Mr. Chala:** Yes, we were once children to.

1. _____
2. _____
3. _____
4. _____
5. _____
6. _____
7. _____

**Proofread Words**  Cross out the homophone that is spelled incorrectly. Write the correct homophone.

8. Everyone cheered when the new queen sat on the thrown.    8. _____

9. Tony beet Alan in the big race.    9. _____

10. Always break at a stop sign.    10. _____

11. Shannon sat bye me at lunch.    11. _____

12. The football star volunteers to read allowed to preschoolers.    12. _____

© Pearson Education, Inc., 4

**Home Activity**  Your child identified misspelled homophones. Ask your child to explain the meaning of several homophones.

34

Name _____

# Vowel Sound in *shout*

| Spelling Words | | | | |
|---|---|---|---|---|
| however | mountain | mound | scout | shout |
| couch | towel | ounce | coward | outdoors |
| flowerpot | scowl | browse | announce | hound |
| trout | drowsy | grouch | eyebrow | boundary |

**Rhymes** Complete each sentence by writing two or more rhyming list words.

"If you (1)___, you'll scare the (2)___," said the (3)___.

1. _____  2. _____  3. _____

Now I can (4)___ that this tennis ball gives the most bounce per (5)___.

4. _____  5. _____

The barking (6)___ jumped over the grassy (7)___.

6. _____  7. _____

The neighborhood (8)___ had nothing nice to say about my comfortable new (9)___.

8. _____  9. _____

"Oh, no. I forgot my beach (10)___," said Jackie with a (11)___.

10. _____  11. _____

**Classifying** Write the list word that best completes each group.

12. seed, soil, ____          12. _____
13. scaredy-cat, chicken, ____   13. _____
14. eyelash, mustache, ____      14. _____
15. sleepy, tired, ____          15. _____
16. in the open, outside, ____   16. _____
17. but, although, ____          17. _____
18. peak, cliff, ____            18. _____
19. look around, glance, ____    19. _____
20. border, margin, ____         20. _____

© Pearson Education, Inc., 4

**Home Activity** Your child wrote words with *ou* and *ow*. Challenge your child to spell the rhyming word groups from the Rhymes exercises on this page.

Name _____

# Vowel Sound in *shout*

**Proofread a Dialogue**  Help Rita correct her dialogue. Circle six misspelled words and write them correctly. Add the missing punctuation mark.

"You said this was a small mownd, but it's a mountain!" grumbled Rita.

"You're such a grouch!" said Andy.

"You don't have to announce it to everyone!" Rita replied.

"We have to do this to get our scowt badge," Chen reminded her.

"But I hate the owtdoors," Rita said with a scoul.

"I know! You'd rather be in your house on the couch," laughed Andy.

"All this walking is making me drousy, said Rita.

"Me, too," agreed Chen. "Let's walk threw the woods and go home."

### Spelling Words

however
mountain
mound
scout
shout
couch
towel
ounce
coward
outdoors

flowerpot
scowl
browse
announce
hound
trout
drowsy
grouch
eyebrow
boundary

1. _____    2. _____
3. _____    4. _____
5. _____    6. _____

**Proofread Words**  Cross out the misspelled word and write it correctly.

### Frequently Misspelled Words

outside
through
house

7. a trawt stream       7. _____
8. a raised eybrow      8. _____
9. a state's boundry line   9. _____
10. a broken flourpot   10. _____
11. a big cowerd        11. _____
12. a nose like a hawnd 12. _____

**Home Activity**  Your child identified misspelled words with *ou* and *ow*. Spell some of the list words aloud. Make some mistakes so your child can correct them.

36

© Pearson Education, Inc., 4

# Compound Words

| Spelling Words | | | | |
|---|---|---|---|---|
| watermelon | homemade | understand | sometimes | shoelace |
| highway | upstairs | thunderstorm | shortcut | doorbell |
| jellyfish | touchdown | campfire | skateboard | anyway |
| fireworks | haircut | loudspeaker | laptop | flashlight |

**Definitions** Write the correct list word beside its definition.

1. portable light powered by batteries
2. hairstyle; trim
3. display of exploding chemicals
4. more direct route; easier way of performing a task
5. occasionally; not in every case
6. main road
7. device to signal that a visitor has arrived
8. clear, transparent marine animal with tentacles
9. outdoor stack of burning wood
10. nevertheless; no matter what

1. _____
2. _____
3. _____
4. _____
5. _____
6. _____
7. _____
8. _____
9. _____
10. _____

**Complete the Sentence** Write a list word to complete each sentence.

11. A cold, juicy slice of ____ tastes great on a hot summer day.
12. Tie that ____ so you don't trip!
13. Mom bakes the most delicious ____ apple pies.
14. Did you hear the announcement that just came over the ____?
15. My ____ computer has a very small screen.
16. I wish I could ride a ____ like my older brother.
17. The team is on the three-yard line and going for a ____.
18. Do you ____ all the rules of the new game?
19. The fourth-grade classroom is ____ on the fourth floor.
20. High winds during the ____ shook the house.

11. _____
12. _____
13. _____
14. _____
15. _____
16. _____
17. _____
18. _____
19. _____
20. _____

© Pearson Education, Inc., 4

**Home Activity** Your child wrote compound words. Have your child draw a vertical line through each word to separate the compound word into its parts.

Name _____

# Compound Words

**Proofread a Schedule** Circle six misspelled words in the camp schedule and write them on the lines. Find the word with a capitalization error and write it correctly.

| Monday | Tuesday | Wednesday | thursday | Friday |
|---|---|---|---|---|
| **Noon** Monkey Walk: Cross a rope highway to get over a stream | **11 A.M.** All About Knots: Bring a long shoe lace | **10 A.M.** Fun with Sound: Sing over the loud speaker | **9 A.M.** Baking: Learn a shortcut for making a shortcake | **10 A.M.** Shave and a Harecut, Two Bits: Fun with shaving cream |
| **5 P.M.** Homade Fudge Tasting | **2 P.M.** Candy Making: Gummy jellyfish | **3 P.M.** Skateboard Contest: Meet on the basketball court | **Noon** Watermelon Seed-Spitting Contest | **Noon** Upload Camp Pictures to the School Laptop |
| **9 P.M.** Flashy Flickers: Bring your flashlite | **5 P.M.** Weather Watch: How to predict a thunderstorm | **9 P.M.** Group Meeting: Meet everywon at the campfire | **9 P.M.** Fireworks | |

1. _____
2. _____
3. _____
4. _____
5. _____
6. _____
7. _____

**Proofread Words** Circle the list word that is spelled correctly. Write the word.

| | | | | |
|---|---|---|---|---|
| **8.** high way | highway | hiway | **8.** _____ |
| **9.** understand | under stand | undestand | **9.** _____ |
| **10.** somtimes | some times | sometimes | **10.** _____ |
| **11.** doorbell | door bell | dorbell | **11.** _____ |
| **12.** upstairs | upstares | up stares | **12.** _____ |

© Pearson Education, Inc., 4

**Home Activity** Your child identified misspelled compound words. Say and spell the first word in a compound list word. Have your child complete the word.

# Possessives

| Spelling Words | | | | |
|---|---|---|---|---|
| its | ours | mine | yours | family's |
| families' | man's | men's | girl's | girls' |
| hers | theirs | brother's | brothers' | teacher's |
| teachers' | aunt's | aunts' | boy's | boys' |

**Words in Context** Complete each pair of sentences by writing the singular or plural possessive form of the word that is to the left of the sentences.

**girl**
1. Both _____ coats were new.
2. That _____ coat looks very warm.

**teacher**
3. I borrowed my _____ pen.
4. The _____ workroom is off-limits to students.

**brother**
5. This is my oldest _____ room.
6. These are my twin _____ rooms.

**family**
7. The party is at the Jackson _____ house.
8. Their driveway is full of other _____ cars.

**aunt**
9. My favorite _____ dog follows her everywhere.
10. My _____ husbands are my uncles.

**boy**
11. The little _____ toy sailboat drifted across the pond.
12. The _____ baseball team plays this afternoon.

1. _____
2. _____
3. _____
4. _____
5. _____
6. _____
7. _____
8. _____
9. _____
10. _____
11. _____
12. _____

**Word Meanings** Write the list word that fits each meaning.

13. belonging to that adult male
14. belonging to an adult female
15. belonging to us
16. belonging to an object
17. belonging to several adult males
18. belonging to me
19. belonging to the person spoken to
20. belonging to those people

13. _____
14. _____
15. _____
16. _____
17. _____
18. _____
19. _____
20. _____

**Home Activity** Your child wrote possessive nouns and pronouns. Have your child tell whether each possessive noun names one person or more than one person.

# Possessives

**Proofread a Newspaper Feature** Proofread the article. Circle six misspelled words and a word with a capitalization error. Write the words correctly on the lines.

**The Smith Family and It's Reunion**

Today was the Smith family's reunion. Seven brothers' families grew to more than one Thousand people in 100 years. The families' cars were parked in a field. The  mens group made special T-shirts for the children. All the girl's shirts had flowers, and the boys' shirts were striped. Everyone laughed and asked, "Yours, ours, or their?" when they looked at the group pictures. The aunt's tent had fifty tables filled with a variety of food. When family members asked who made each dish, the women laughed, pointed at each other, and said, "It's hers." At the end of the day, everyone said, "That's enouf! I can't eat another thing!"

1. _____  2. _____
3. _____  4. _____
5. _____  6. _____
7. _____

**Possessives** Add apostrophes to the underlined words. Write the possessives correctly on the lines.

8. the <u>families</u> yards        8. _____
9. my <u>teachers</u> desk          9. _____
10. the <u>mans</u> hat             10. _____
11. my <u>brothers</u> toothbrushes 11. _____
12. the <u>girls</u> bicycle        12. _____

**Home Activity** Your child identified misspelled possessive nouns and pronouns. Have your child use the possessive pronouns in sentences.

# Adding *-ed* and *-ing*

### Spelling Words

| | | | | |
|---|---|---|---|---|
| watched | watching | danced | dancing | studied |
| studying | stopped | stopping | dried | drying |
| happened | happening | noticed | noticing | robbed |
| robbing | slipped | slipping | hurried | hurrying |

**Watch the Changes** Write the *-ed* and the *-ing* form for each word. Circle the list words that change the spelling of the base form.

dance      1. _____      2. _____

dry      3. _____      4. _____

happen      5. _____      6. _____

hurry      7. _____      8. _____

notice      9. _____      10. _____

rob      11. _____      12. _____

stop      13. _____      14. _____

slip      15. _____      16. _____

study      17. _____      18. _____

watch      19. _____      20. _____

© Pearson Education, Inc., 4

**Home Activity** Your child learned to spell words with *-ed* and *-ing* endings. Ask your child to spell list words and explain what ending was added.

# Homophones

| Spelling Words | | | | |
|---|---|---|---|---|
| two | to | too | piece | peace |
| break | brake | there | their | they're |
| threw | through | by | bye | beat |
| beet | thrown | throne | aloud | allowed |

**Words in Context** Write the list word whose meaning best fits each sentence.

1. The _____ is a remarkable vegetable.
2. The children handed in _____ papers.
3. After working an hour, we were ready for a _____.
4. I would like a _____ of pumpkin pie.
5. The queen rested on her _____.
6. The class likes it when Mr. Fox reads _____.
7. You should be home _____ 5 p.m.
8. Tara _____ us all in the race.
9. The ball crashed _____ the window.
10. The shortstop has _____ the ball to the catcher.

1. _____
2. _____
3. _____
4. _____
5. _____
6. _____
7. _____
8. _____
9. _____
10. _____

**Definitions** Circle the word that fits each definition. Then write the word.

| | | | |
|---|---|---|---|
| 11. in that place | their | there | 11. _____ |
| 12. permitted | allowed | aloud | 12. _____ |
| 13. calm silence | peace | piece | 13. _____ |
| 14. used for stopping | brake | break | 14. _____ |
| 15. farewell | by | bye | 15. _____ |
| 16. also | two | too | 16. _____ |
| 17. they are | their | they're | 17. _____ |
| 18. rhythm of music | beat | beet | 18. _____ |
| 19. tossed | threw | through | 19. _____ |
| 20. monarch's seat | throne | thrown | 20. _____ |

© Pearson Education, Inc., 4

**Home Activity** Your child has learned word pairs that sound the same but have different spellings and meanings. Challenge your child to use each pair of homophones in a single sentence.

# Vowel Sound in *shout*

**Spelling Words**

| | | | | |
|---|---|---|---|---|
| however | mountain | mound | scout | shout |
| couch | towel | ounce | coward | outdoors |
| flowerpot | scowl | browse | announce | hound |
| trout | drowsy | grouch | eyebrow | boundary |

**Match Up** Draw a line connecting two word parts that form a list word.

1. moun        brow

2. flower       tain

3. eye         nounce

4. out         sy

5. boun        ever

6. how        dary

7. drow       doors

8. an         pot

**Word Search** Find the list words from the box hidden in the puzzle. Words are down, across, and diagonal.

```
B Z S C O U T K M C B G
X R H N I V R P O O S R
A H O U N D O A U W I O
C O U W B C U E N A V U
V W T I S D T Q D R U C
K N M P C E K O K D M H
Z D I Q O O X U I Y N E
E H F C W Z U N A T R R
T O W E L Y O C J T S X
J K L Z Q Y I E H P A E
```

| |
|---|
| scout |
| towel |
| hound |
| grouch |
| mound |
| trout |
| ounce |
| shout |
| scowl |
| couch |
| browse |
| coward |

**Home Activity** Your child learned words with /ou/ spelled *ou* and *ow*. Write each list word leaving blanks where the *ou* or *ow* belong. Ask your child to complete each word.

# Compound Words

| Spelling Words | | | | |
|---|---|---|---|---|
| watermelon | homemade | understand | sometimes | shoelace |
| highway | upstairs | thunderstorm | shortcut | doorbell |
| jellyfish | touchdown | campfire | skateboard | anyway |
| fireworks | haircut | loudspeaker | laptop | flashlight |

**Double Clues** Each item gives two clues for small words. Write the list word made by adding the smaller words together.

1. for your foot + string
2. put on toast + swims in water
3. on your head + snip with scissors
4. not down + passage to second story
5. sleep outdoors + light with a match
6. opening into house + ringer
7. not low + route
8. liquid to drink + large fruit
9. not quiet + one who talks
10. booming noise + big wind

1. _____
2. _____
3. _____
4. _____
5. _____
6. _____
7. _____
8. _____
9. _____
10. _____

**Proofread Words** Circle the misspelled list word in each sentence. Write the word correctly.

11. The park sets off firewurks on July 4th.
12. We had a flaslight in our tent.
13. If you do not unnerstand, ask questions.
14. These pies are homade by Uncle Tim.
15. It rained, but we went for a walk enyway.
16. Do you have a laptope or a desktop computer?
17. The football team scored a tuchdown.
18. I sumtimes eat dessert before dinner.
19. Damien can do tricks on his scatboard.
20. We took a shortkut through the woods.

11. _____
12. _____
13. _____
14. _____
15. _____
16. _____
17. _____
18. _____
19. _____
20. _____

© Pearson Education, Inc., 4

**School + Home** **Home Activity** Your child learned compound words. Write each list word on a paper strip. Have your child cut the two words apart. Mix strips and have your child reform the words.

# Possessives

| Spelling Words | | | | |
|---|---|---|---|---|
| its | ours | mine | yours | family's |
| families' | man's | men's | girl's | girls' |
| hers | theirs | brother's | brothers' | teacher's |
| teachers' | aunt's | aunts' | boy's | boys' |

**Who Owns It?** Write the list word pronoun that fits in each box.

| BELONGING TO | ONE OWNER | TWO OR MORE OWNERS |
|---|---|---|
| AN OBJECT | 1. | ██████ |
| A FEMALE | 2. | ██████ |
| PERSON/PEOPLE SPOKEN TO | 3. | 3. |
| YOU AND ME | ██████ | 4. |
| ME | 5. | ██████ |
| THOSE PEOPLE | ██████ | 6. |

**Singular or Plural?** Write the possessive forms of each noun.

| NOUN | SINGULAR POSSESSIVE | PLURAL POSSESSIVE |
|---|---|---|
| family | 7. | 8. |
| teacher | 9. | 10. |
| man | 11. | 12. |
| girl | 13. | 14. |
| brother | 15. | 16. |
| aunt | 17. | 18. |
| boy | 19. | 20. |

**Home Activity** Your child learned to spell singular and plural possessives. Use each word in a sentence and have your child spell it correctly.

© Pearson Education, Inc., 4

Name _____

# Contractions

| Spelling Words | | | | |
|---|---|---|---|---|
| don't | won't | wouldn't | there's | we're |
| you're | doesn't | I've | here's | wasn't |
| shouldn't | couldn't | where's | hadn't | aren't |
| they're | it's | we've | when's | haven't |

**Familiar Sayings** Write the contraction that correctly completes each saying.

1. _____ count your chickens before they hatch.
2. People in glass houses _____ throw stones.
3. _____ no time like the present.
4. _____ as alike as two peas in a pod.
5. _____ the time gone?
6. _____ the thought that counts.

1. _____
2. _____
3. _____
4. _____
5. _____
6. _____

**Contractions** Write the contraction that can be made from the underlined words.

7. The band was so loud I <u>could not</u> hear you.
8. The kindergartners <u>have not</u> visited the zoo yet.
9. Carrie <u>will not</u> be here today because she is sick.
10. <u>When is</u> our next club meeting?
11. <u>You are</u> right on time!
12. <u>Here is</u> my homework assignment.
13. Lisa was so angry she <u>would not</u> speak to me all day.
14. We <u>are not</u> old enough to drive.
15. The actor <u>was not</u> sure he knew his lines.
16. Before today, Kim <u>had not</u> played softball.
17. <u>I have</u> been taking dancing lessons for five years.
18. Do you know when <u>we are</u> leaving?
19. Jennifer <u>does not</u> have any pets.
20. Do you want to know where <u>we have</u> been?

7. _____
8. _____
9. _____
10. _____
11. _____
12. _____
13. _____
14. _____
15. _____
16. _____
17. _____
18. _____
19. _____
20. _____

© Pearson Education, Inc., 4

**Home Activity** Your child wrote contractions. Have your child tell which letters were replaced by the apostrophe in each contraction.

# Contractions

**Proofread Riddles** Circle six spelling errors in Vicki's list of riddles. Write the words correctly on the lines. Rewrite the sentence that ends with the wrong punctuation mark.

Why don't rivers go out of style?
Because theyr'e always current!

When'is fishing not a good way to relax?
When you're a worm!

Wheres' the ocean the deepest?
At the bottom.

What driver does't need a license.
A screwdriver!

Why should you wear a watch in the desert?
Because there's a spring inside.

Why woudn't the letter E spend any money?
Because its always in debt.

1. _____     2. _____
3. _____     4. _____
5. _____     6. _____
7. _____

**Missing Words** Circle the contraction that is spelled correctly. Write it.

8. **We've   We'ev**   chosen you for our team.          8. _____

9. There **ar'nt   aren't**   any more books on the shelf.   9. _____

10. The puppy **wouldn't   woodn't**   come when I called.   10. _____

11. **Hear's   Here's**   my missing shoe!                11. _____

12. Nick **doesn't   dosen't**   like ice cream.           12. _____

**Home Activity** Your child identified misspelled contractions. Write each contraction, omitting the apostrophes. Have your child add the missing apostrophe to each word.

Name _____

# Final Syllable Patterns

| Spelling Words | | | | |
|---|---|---|---|---|
| chicken | natural | several | paddle | oval |
| eleven | together | summer | animal | frighten |
| brother | calendar | threaten | pitcher | mumble |
| jungle | needle | caterpillar | shelter | deliver |

**Word Groups** Write the list word that best completes each word group.

1. turkey, goose, ____

2. murmur, mutter, ____

3. joined, with, ____

4. winter, spring, ____

5. elliptical, egg-shaped, ____

6. cocoon, butterfly, ____

7. usual, normal, ____

8. many, numerous, ____

9. row, oar, ____

10. startle, scare, ____

1. _____
2. _____
3. _____
4. _____
5. _____
6. _____
7. _____
8. _____
9. _____
10. _____

**Missing Words** Write a list word to complete the sentence.

11. Turn to a new page on the ____.

12. When the rain came, we took ____ in the library.

13. My little sister will ____ to run away if she gets angry.

14. Please fill the ____ with water.

15. The number ____ is one more than ten.

16. The driver will ____ the packages to the airport.

17. A domestic ____ lives with people.

18. It takes some skill to get thread through the eye of a ____.

19. My baby ____ will cry out when he is hungry.

20. Monkeys swing from tree to tree in the ____.

11. _____
12. _____
13. _____
14. _____
15. _____
16. _____
17. _____
18. _____
19. _____
20. _____

© Pearson Education, Inc., 4

**School + Home**

**Home Activity** Your child wrote words that end with *le, al, en, ar,* and *er*. Have your child identify the five list words that are most difficult for him or her, spell the words, and use them in sentences.

# Final Syllable Patterns

**Proofread a Story** Melissa is writing a story. Proofread her first paragraph. Circle six spelling errors. Write the words correctly. Find a run-on sentence and write it correctly.

© Pearson Education, Inc., 4

---

### The Mysterious Path

All elevin students zigzagged in a path across the wet field. Then they entered a forest that was as dark as a jungal the students had to walk through the tangle of bushes in a single line. Every thorn scratched like a needel. Even though the students tried to hold their voices to a soft mumbel, they couldn't help but frightan some of the animals. An aminal ran across their path and snarled, trying to threaten these strange people.

---

**Spelling Words**

chicken
eleven
brother
jungle
natural
together
calendar
needle
several
summer

threaten
caterpillar
paddle
animal
pitcher
shelter
oval
frighten
mumble
deliver

1. _____    2. _____

3. _____    4. _____

5. _____    6. _____

7. _____

_____

_____

**Frequently Misspelled Words**

people
hospital
another

**Proofread Words** Fill in the circle beside the word that is spelled correctly. Write the word.

8. ○ ovel        ○ oval        ○ ovle        8. _____

9. ○ naturall     ○ naturale     ○ natural      9. _____

10. ○ deliver     ○ dilever      ○ diliver      10. _____

11. ○ pither      ○ pitcher      ○ pitcer       11. _____

12. ○ frigten     ○ frighten     ○ frightten    12. _____

**Home Activity** Your child identified misspelled words that end with *le*, *al*, *ar*, *er*, and *en*. Say list words that end with the schwa-*l* sound and have your child tell whether the final syllable is spelled with an *le* or *al*.

# Consonant Digraph /sh/

| Spelling Words | | | | |
|---|---|---|---|---|
| nation | special | lotion | mansion | precious |
| creation | vacation | tension | especially | motion |
| tradition | gracious | extension | addition | caution |
| official | solution | suspension | politician | portion |

**Missing Words** Write the list word that completes the sentence.

1. The telephone was a very helpful ____.

2. I have devised a ____ to our problem.

3. The wealthy surgeon lives in the ____ on the hill.

4. Please bring an extra bottle of ____ to the beach.

5. You have certainly earned your ____ of the prize.

6. We are studying the laws of ____ in physics class.

7. There are fifty states in our ____.

8. The Golden Gate Bridge is a huge ____ bridge.

9. In ____ to his speech, he presented a demonstration.

10. My family once took a _____ to Hawaii.

1. _____
2. _____
3. _____
4. _____
5. _____
6. _____
7. _____
8. _____
9. _____
10. _____

**Categorizing** Write the list word that completes each word group.

11. unusual, unique, ____

12. valuable, prized, ____

13. stress, pressure, ____

14. mainly, particularly, ____

15. custom, ritual, ____

16. senator, president, ____

17. concern, care, ____

18. executive, representative, ____

19. expansion, addition, ____

20. sociable, cordial, ____

11. _____
12. _____
13. _____
14. _____
15. _____
16. _____
17. _____
18. _____
19. _____
20. _____

© Pearson Education, Inc., 4

**School + Home**

**Home Activity** Your child wrote words with the sound /sh/. Say the /sh/ words, and ask your child to spell them.

# Consonant Digraph /sh/

**Proofread a Speech** Circle six misspelled words in the speech. Write the words correctly. Write the sentence with a verb in the incorrect tense correctly.

> Holiday Vacasion Packages!
>
> Fly anywhere in the nashion. We have the best rates! Book your flight now and get a free 2-night extention at America's offishal hotel of choice. Our gratious flight attendants will make you feel at home. Call now and a porshion of your cost will be donates to Charity.

1. _____  2. _____  3. _____

4. _____  5. _____  6. _____

7. _____
   _____

**Proofread Words** Circle the list word in each sentence that is spelled correctly.

**8.** My mother is a very **speshial** **special** person.

**9.** We made an interesting **creation** **creacion** in science class.

**10.** Mr. Buck is building an **addishion** **addition** to the school.

**11.** Always use **caution** **causion** when swimming at the lake.

**12.** My mountain bike is my most **pretious** **precious** belonging.

**Spelling Words**

nation
special
lotion
mansion
precious
creation
vacation
tension
especially
motion

tradition
gracious
extension
addition
caution
official
solution
suspension
politician
portion

**Frequently Misspelled Words**

let's
that's

© Pearson Education, Inc., 4

**Home Activity** Your child identified misspelled words with the sound /sh/. Misspell the list words your child did not use on this page, and have your child correct them.

# Consonants /j/, /ks/, and /kw/

| Spelling Words | | | | |
|---|---|---|---|---|
| village | except | explain | quick | charge |
| bridge | knowledge | question | equal | queen |
| excited | expect | Texas | fudge | excellent |
| exercise | quart | liquid | quilt | expert |

**Missing Words** Write the list word that completes the sentence.

1. The capital of _____ is Austin.

2. Some books are full of information, learning, and _____.

3. Stores and places of business are found in the _____.

4. The royal subjects bowed before the _____.

5. A good rainy day activity is making chocolate _____.

6. Two pints are equal to one _____.

7. A lot of work goes into making a handmade _____.

8. Water is a colorless, odorless, tasteless _____.

9. A healthy diet and _____ is the path to good health.

10. Four quarts are _____ to one gallon.

11. The _____ was built over the sparkling river.

12. We were _____ to go to the amusement park.

1. _____
2. _____
3. _____
4. _____
5. _____
6. _____
7. _____
8. _____
9. _____
10. _____
11. _____
12. _____

**Categorizing** Write the list word that completes each word group.

13. outstanding, superb, _____

14. but, excluding, _____

15. ask, query, _____

16. cost, fee, _____

17. describe, clarify, _____

18. fast, speedy, _____

19. specialist, authority, _____

20. demand, await, _____

13. _____
14. _____
15. _____
16. _____
17. _____
18. _____
19. _____
20. _____

© Pearson Education, Inc., 4

**School + Home**

**Home Activity** Your child wrote words spelled with with consonants /j/, /ks/, and /kw/. Say those words and ask your child to spell them.

# Consonants /j/, /ks/, and /kw/

**Proofread an Ad** Ed wants the newspaper ad about his gas station to be perfect. Circle the six misspelled words and write them correctly. Circle the word with a capitalization error and write it correctly.

Spelling Words

| Spelling Words |
|---|
| village |
| except |
| explain |
| quick |
| charge |
| bridge |
| knowledge |
| question |
| equal |
| queen |
| |
| excited |
| expect |
| Texas |
| fudge |
| excellent |
| exercise |
| quart |
| liquid |
| quilt |
| expert |

> Drive into Ed's Gas Station!
>
> We have the lowest gas prices in the village.
>
> Try us for a qwick oil change or tire repair.
>
> We offer eggscellent repair and exspert service.
>
> Ask us any question about your car.
>
> We have knowledge about every make and model car.
>
> We explane the problem to you before we fix it.
>
> Your car will be fit for a king or qween.
>
> Open everyday exsept sunday.

1. _____  2. _____  3. _____

4. _____  5. _____  6. _____

7. _____

**Proofread Words** Circle the misspelled list word. Write it correctly.

8. Everyone was ekscited when the circus came to town.

8. _____

9. The class will expand their knowlej about other countries.

9. _____

10. The brige was closed for construction.

10. _____

11. There was no admission chardge for students.

11. _____

12. All team members get equel playing time.

12. _____

| Frequently Misspelled Words |
|---|
| except |
| off |
| something |

**Home Activity** Your child identified misspelled words with the sound /j/, /ks/, and /kw/. Misspell the list words your child did not use on this page, and have your child correct them.

# Prefixes *un-*, *dis-*, *in-*

| Spelling Words | | | | |
|---|---|---|---|---|
| distrust | uncertain | incomplete | unlikely | unfair |
| discontinue | unaware | disorder | discount | indirect |
| unopened | disrespect | unimportant | unlisted | disrepair |
| inability | disapprove | unsolved | disobey | unsuspecting |

**Add Prefixes** Write the list word that can replace the underlined words.

1. The mystery of the missing book is still <u>not solved</u>.

2. My best friend's phone number is <u>not listed</u>.

3. We decided to <u>not continue</u> the newspaper delivery.

4. We <u>do not trust</u> people who do not tell the truth.

5. It's seven o'clock, and my homework is still <u>not complete</u>.

6. It's <u>not likely</u> that we'll see a flying elephant anytime soon.

7. The new box of cookies is <u>not opened</u>.

8. The puppy does not mean to <u>not obey</u>.

9. The outcome of the contest is still <u>not certain</u>.

1. _____

2. _____

3. _____

4. _____

5. _____

6. _____

7. _____

8. _____

9. _____

**Synonyms** Write a list word that has the same or almost the same meaning as the clues.

10. not suspicious

11. ignorant

12. mess

13. rudeness

14. roundabout

15. unjust

16. insignificant

17. not in working order

18. money off

19. turn down

20. lack of skill

10. _____

11. _____

12. _____

13. _____

14. _____

15. _____

16. _____

17. _____

18. _____

19. _____

20. _____

© Pearson Education, Inc., 4

**School + Home**

**Home Activity** Your child wrote words with prefixes *un-*, *dis-*, and *in-*. Say base words. Ask your child to add a prefix to say the list word.

54

Name _____

# Prefixes *un-*, *dis-*, *in-*

**Proofread a Letter** Circle seven misspelled words in the letter. Write the words correctly. Add the missing punctuation mark.

Dear Mayor

It seems that you are inaware of the state of the city playground. The workers seem to have discontined their work, even though the project is still uncomplete. There is inorder everywhere. It appears that you think the needs of children are immmportant. We think it is best that you keep this unsafe place to play disopened untill everything is fixed.

Yours truly,
The Fourth-Grade Class

### Spelling Words

distrust
uncertain
incomplete
unlikely
unfair
discontinue
unaware
disorder
discount
indirect

unopened
disrespect
unimportant
unlisted
disrepair
inability
disapprove
unsolved
disobey
unsuspecting

1. _____   2. _____   3. _____

4. _____   5. _____   6. _____

7. _____

**Missing Words** Circle the letter of the word that is spelled correctly. Write the word.

### Frequently Misspelled Words

until
into
unfair
disappear
invisible

**8.** I love finding bargains at the _____ store.
   A. discont    B. discount    C. miscount

**9.** I am _____ of the exact directions to the museum.
   A. uncertan    B. incertain    C. uncertain

**10.** In the _____ event of a flood, go up the hill.
   A. unlikly    B. unlikey    C. unlikely

**11.** Why does your dog always _____ your commands?
   A. disobey    B. disobay    C. diobey

**12.** I have an _____ to keep a knapsack neat and in order.
   A. unability    B. inability    C. inabilty

8. _____

9. _____

10. _____

11. _____

12. _____

**Home Activity** Your child identified misspelled words with prefixes *un-*, *dis-*, and *in-*. Say a prefix and have your child name list words that begin with the prefix.

55

Name _____

# Contractions

**Proofread Contractions** Circle the list word that is spelled incorrectly.

1. The clothes havn't dried.

2. They dont' know the answer.

3. Some campers are'nt prepared.

4. Your halfway up the mountain.

5. That noise wasnot' familiar.

6. Campers shuldn't wander off.

7. Were hoping to reach the top.

8. Tomorrow their going home.

9. Whens breakfast going to be served?

10. Its way too hot to climb.

**Proofread Contractions** The underlined word in each sentence is incorrect. Write the corrected list word.

11. They <u>had'nt</u> put out the fire.

12. <u>Her's</u> a bucket for water.

13. Max <u>culdn't</u> make the cocoa.

14. This stew <u>duzn't</u> look done.

15. <u>Theirs</u> a strong breeze off the lake.

16. The trail <u>wont</u> be open after a storm.

17. The wet wood <u>would'nt</u> catch fire.

18. After <u>we'ave</u> set up, we can rest.

19. <u>Ive</u> had a lot of fun on this trip.

20. <u>Were's</u> my backpack?

11. _____

12. _____

13. _____

14. _____

15. _____

16. _____

17. _____

18. _____

19. _____

20. _____

© Pearson Education, Inc., 4

**Home Activity** Your child learned to spell contractions. Read each sentence on this page and have your child spell the contraction in it correctly.

56

# Final Syllable Patterns

Name _____

| Spelling Words | | | | |
|---|---|---|---|---|
| chicken | natural | several | paddle | oval |
| eleven | together | summer | animal | frighten |
| brother | calendar | threaten | pitcher | mumble |
| jungle | needle | caterpillar | shelter | deliver |

**Analogies** Write the list word that best completes the comparison.

1. Horse is to foal as _____ is to chick.
2. Help is to hurt as protect is to _____.
3. Bike is to pedal as canoe is to _____.
4. Bison is to prairie as monkey is to _____.
5. One is to two as ten is to _____.
6. Girl is to boy as sister is to _____.
7. Teddy bear is to bear as fake is to _____.
8. Hot is to cold as _____ is to winter.
9. Square is to rectangle as circle is to _____.
10. Delight is to please as scare is to _____.

1. _____
2. _____
3. _____
4. _____
5. _____
6. _____
7. _____
8. _____
9. _____
10. _____

**Definitions** Write the list word that fits the definition.

11. a few; more than one
12. joined; not separate
13. to drop off an object at some location
14. a chart showing days in a year
15. a structure that protects from rain and snow
16. an insect that becomes a butterfly
17. a living being that is not a plant
18. to speak in a low, unclear way
19. a container from which a liquid is poured
20. a thin metal rod with a hole in one end

11. _____
12. _____
13. _____
14. _____
15. _____
16. _____
17. _____
18. _____
19. _____
20. _____

**Home Activity** Your child spelled words that end with *le, al, en, ar,* and *er*. Use each list word in a sentence and have your child spell it aloud.

# Consonant Digraph /sh/

| Spelling Words | | | | |
| --- | --- | --- | --- | --- |
| nation | special | lotion | mansion | precious |
| creation | vacation | tension | especially | motion |
| tradition | gracious | extension | addition | caution |
| official | solution | suspension | politician | portion |

**Word Meanings** Write the list word that fits the definition.

1. something that is made
2. cream for your skin
3. person who runs for office
4. important or valuable
5. a segment or piece of something
6. answer or resolution
7. a part that makes something longer or larger
8. representative or high-ranking person
9. tightness or strain
10. extraordinary or unusual
11. a routine or ritual
12. holiday or break from work

1. _____
2. _____
3. _____
4. _____
5. _____
6. _____
7. _____
8. _____
9. _____
10. _____
11. _____
12. _____

**Analogies** Write the list word that best completes the comparison.

13. Village is to town as _____ is to country.
14. Largely is to greatly as particularly is to _____.
15. Unfriendly is to unsociable as friendly is to _____.
16. Hurry is to rush as delay is to _____.
17. Car is to limousine as house is to _____.
18. Plus is to minus as _____ is to subtraction.
19. Act is to action as move is to _____.
20. Haste is to careless as _____ is to careful.

13. _____
14. _____
15. _____
16. _____
17. _____
18. _____
19. _____
20. _____

**Home Activity** Your child learned words with the sound /sh/. Have your child identify list words that give him or her trouble. Have a joke-writing contest using these words.

Name _____

# Consonants /j/, /ks/, and /kw/

## Spelling Words

| | | | | |
|---|---|---|---|---|
| village | except | explain | quick | charge |
| bridge | knowledge | question | equal | queen |
| excited | expect | Texas | fudge | excellent |
| exercise | quart | liquid | quilt | expert |

**Word Meanings** Write the list word that fits the definition.

1. royal female ruler of a country
2. one fourth of a gallon
3. something asked that needs an answer
4. having the same amount, size, elements
5. bed covering patterned from cloth pieces
6. rich chocolate candy
7. small town in the country
8. structure built over water
9. done in a short time
10. matter that pours
11. to ask for as a price
12. what a person knows or understands

1. _____
2. _____
3. _____
4. _____
5. _____
6. _____
7. _____
8. _____
9. _____
10. _____
11. _____
12. _____

**The *ex's* Have It** Write the list words with *ex* to complete each sentence.

13. That is an _____ idea you had.
14. Everyone will go _____ Harry. He will stay here.
15. The class was _____ to see a deer in the playground.
16. You can skate or swim to get _____.
17. Your teachers _____ you to do your best.
18. Mr. Washington is an _____ on snakes.
19. Bree asked the teacher to _____ how bees fly.
20. The largest southern state is _____.

13. _____
14. _____
15. _____
16. _____
17. _____
18. _____
19. _____
20. _____

**Home Activity** Your child learned words with consonants /j/, /ks/, and /kw/. Have your child identify list words that give him or her trouble. Have a joke-writing contest using these words.

# Prefixes un-, dis-, in-

**Missing Words** Write a list word with *un-* to complete each sentence.

1. It is _____ to snow in July.
2. There are _____ cans of food in the pantry.
3. It would be _____ to give everyone a trophy.
4. Marie was _____ which coat to buy.
5. Our family phone number is _____.
6. The star detective leaves no case _____.
7. An _____ homeowner was about to be robbed.
8. The robber was _____ that the police lay in wait.
9. No detail was _____ to the police.

1. _____
2. _____
3. _____
4. _____
5. _____
6. _____
7. _____
8. _____
9. _____

**Antonyms** Write a *dis-* list word that means the opposite, or nearly the opposite, of each word or phrase.

10. shipshape _____
11. carry on _____
12. do what you're told _____
13. have faith in _____
14. overcharge _____
15. admiration _____
16. neatness _____
17. give your support _____

**Word Scramble** Unscramble the list words and write the letters on the lines.

18. blainiiyt _____
19. moctleepin _____
20. nictreid _____

# Multisyllabic Words

Spelling Words

reaction
prerecorded
incorrectly
incredibly
disobedient
disagreeable
refreshment
unbreakable
declaration
retirement

misdialed
undefined
unhappily
watchfully
gleefully
sportsmanship
repayment
questionable
displacement
midshipman

**Antonyms** Write a list word that has the opposite or almost the opposite meaning.

1. pleasant          1. _____

2. joyfully          2. _____

3. inattentively     3. _____

4. unfairness        4. _____

5. certain           5. _____

6. unexceptionally   6. _____

**Synonyms** Write the list word that has the same or almost the same meaning.

7. statement                  7. _____

8. called the wrong number    8. _____

9. career's end               9. _____

10. relocation               10. _____

**Definitions** Replace the underlined words with list words that mean the same thing.

11. You can call a number to listen to a <u>taped</u> message that tells the movie schedule.          11. _____

12. The <u>food</u> committee served cookies and lemonade.          12. _____

13. We sang the silly song <u>cheerfully</u>.          13. _____

14. The <u>naval cadet</u> mopped the deck.          14. _____

15. The figures in the painting are blurry and <u>vague</u>.          15. _____

16. My <u>response</u> to eating tomatoes is hives and puffy eyes.          16. _____

17. I <u>mistakenly</u> gave credit to the wrong person.          17. _____

18. Fortunately, the glass I dropped is <u>indestructible</u>!          18. _____

19. I returned the shoes, and I'm waiting for my <u>refund</u> check.          19. _____

20. Our <u>naughty</u> dog failed at puppy training school!          20. _____

**Home Activity** Your child wrote multisyllabic words. Have your child spell the list words syllable by syllable.

# Multisyllabic Words

**Proofread an Anecdote** Read Amy's story. Circle six misspelled words. Write the words correctly. Circle a punctuation mistake and write the sentence correctly.

reaction
prerecorded
incorrectly
incredibly
disobedient
disagreeable
refreshment
unbreakable
declaration
retirement

misdialed
undefined
unhappily
watchfully
gleefully
sportsmanship
repayment
questionable
displacement
midshipman

### An Awful Day

My cousin was coming for a visit? I decided to order a pizza. I misdiled the number and got a precorded message from an insurance company. Then I dialed incorectly again! Finally, I placed my order. When my cousin saw the pizza, she made a startling declaration. She said she never eats pizza because she gets an allergic raction from tomatoes. We had an incredably awful dinner. Im going to go back to bed!

1. _____  2. _____  3. _____

4. _____  5. _____  6. _____

7. _____

**Proofread Words** Circle the letter of the word that is spelled correctly. Write the word.

8. My cat waited _____ as I prepared her meal.
   A. wachfully      B. watchfily      C. watchfully

9. Olympic athletes are expected to practice good _____.
   A. sportsmanship   B. sportsmenship   C. sportmanship

10. Adding ice cubes causes _____ of the liquid in the glass.
    A. displacment     B. displacement    C. displacemant

11. A villain's motives are always _____.
    A. questonable     B. questinible     C. questionable

12. His _____ behavior is usually punished.
    A. disobedient     B. disobediant     C. disobedint

8. _____
9. _____
10. _____
11. _____
12. _____

**School + Home**

**Home Activity** Your child identified misspelled multisyllabic words. Have your child draw vertical lines to divide the list words into syllables.

# Words with Double Consonants

### Spelling Words

| | | | | |
|---|---|---|---|---|
| tomorrow | borrow | different | rabbit | matter |
| written | bottle | ridden | odd | bubble |
| offer | suffer | slippers | grasshopper | worry |
| current | lettuce | saddle | shudder | hobby |

**Word Groups** Write the list word that best completes each word group.

1. yesterday, today, ___
2. raccoon, rat, ___
3. shake, tremble, ___
4. leafy, salad, ___
5. can, container, ___
6. give, present, ___
7. horse, stirrups, ___
8. etched, typed, ___
9. ladybug, butterfly, ___
10. shoes, sandals, ___

1. _____
2. _____
3. _____
4. _____
5. _____
6. _____
7. _____
8. _____
9. _____
10. _____

**Missing Words** Complete each sentence by writing a list word.

11. Please don't ____ about the spilled milk.
12. May I ____ your extra raincoat?
13. My cat was behaving in a rather ____ manner.
14. Do you have the ____ issue of this magazine?
15. Every person is ____ in his or her own way.
16. Building model cars is my grandfather's new ____.
17. My father continues to ____ with the flu.
18. Now we can get down to the heart of the ____.
19. I have never ____ such a tall horse.
20. My friends like to see who can blow the biggest ____.

11. _____
12. _____
13. _____
14. _____
15. _____
16. _____
17. _____
18. _____
19. _____
20. _____

© Pearson Education, Inc., 4

**Home Activity** Your child wrote words with double consonants. Have your child explain how double consonants stand for one sound.

# Words with Double Consonants

**Proofread a Speech** Circle six misspelled words in the speech. Write the words correctly. Write the sentence with a verb in the incorrect tense correctly.

Welcome, Friends of the Zoo! I'd like to thank all of you who kindly ofer your time to our local zoo. Tomorow is Family Education Day at the zoo. An expert will talk about the cicada, grasshoper, and beetle. Children can learn what makes them diferent. You can also feed letuce to a rabit in the petting zoo. Again, I want to thanks you all for your support.

1. _____
2. _____
3. _____
4. _____
5. _____
6. _____
7. _____

**Proofread Words** Circle the list word in each sentence that is spelled correctly.

8. What is the **matter    mater**  with Andy's parakeet?

9. Have you ever **ridden    riden**  in a hot air balloon?

10. At night, I like to wear my comfortable **slipers    slippers**.

11. Please take an extra **bottle    botle**  of water.

12. My sister is letting me **borrow    borow**  her grey sweater.

© Pearson Education, Inc., 4

**School + Home**

**Home Activity** Your child identified misspelled words with double consonants. Spell the first syllable of a list word and have your child spell the rest of the word.

Name _____

# Greek Word Parts

**Word Groups** Write the list word that best fits into each group.

1. topic sentence, supporting sentences, ___     1. _____
2. life story, nonfiction, ___                   2. _____
3. bacteria, lens, ___                           3. _____
4. film, camera, ___                             4. _____
5. oven, rapid, ___                              5. _____
6. voice, record, ___                            6. _____
7. instrument, woodwind, ___                     7. _____
8. signature, celebrity, ___                     8. _____
9. universe, lens, ___                           9. _____
10. weather, air pressure, ___                   10. _____

**Missing Word** Write the list word that best completes each sentence.

11. A ____ is shaped like a cone.
12. A ____ is a tiny processor inside a computer.
13. A ____ allows sailors in a submarine to see above water.
14. Measure across the center of a circle to find its ____.
15. Morse code, a series of dots and dashes, was sent by ____.
16. A full ____ orchestra has strings, woodwinds, brass, and percussion sections.
17. Wear ____ when you don't want to disturb others in the room.
18. To find the ____, measure the sides of a shape and add them together.
19. Beginning readers learn to use ____ to sound out new words.
20. Alexander Graham Bell invented the ____.

11. _____
12. _____
13. _____
14. _____
15. _____
16. _____
17. _____
18. _____
19. _____
20. _____

**Home Activity** Your child wrote words with Greek word parts. Ask your child to use the meanings of the Greek word parts to help define the words.

Name _____

# Greek Word Parts

**Proofread an Assignment** Sam quickly copied his teacher's assignment. Circle six misspelled words and one word with a capitalization error. Write the words correctly.

© Pearson Education, Inc., 4

> Class Assignment: Write a six-paragraph biografy of one of these famous people.
>
> Alexander Graham Bell, inventor of the telaphone
>
> Ludwig van Beethoven, Symphony composer
>
> Anton van Leeuwenhoek, inventor of the microscope
>
> Galileo and the telesope
>
> Charlie "Bird" Parker, great saxaphone player
>
> Jack Kilby, inventor of the microchip
>
> Percy Spencer, inventor of the micrawave oven
>
> Simon Lake, periscope inventor
>
> Teddy Roosevelt, President and frend of nature
>
> Evangelista Torricelli, inventor of the barometer

**Spelling Words**

telephone
biography
telescope
photograph
microwave
diameter
barometer
microscope
headphones
microphone

autograph
microchip
telegraph
perimeter
paragraph
phonics
symphony
saxophone
periscope
megaphone

1. _____    2. _____
3. _____    4. _____
5. _____    6. _____
7. _____

**Frequently Misspelled Words**

friend
then

**Proofread Words** Circle the list word that is spelled correctly.

| | | | |
|---|---|---|---|
| 8. microphone | microfone | 9. phonics | phonicks |
| 10. peremeter | perimeter | 11. magaphone | megaphone |
| 12. autograff | autograph | 13. telegraph | teligraph |
| 14. diameter | diamiter | 15. perescope | periscope |

**Home Activity** Your child identified misspelled words with Greek word parts. Have your child find and circle two letters that stand for the sound of *f* in the list words.

Name _____

# Latin Roots

| Spelling Words | | | | |
|---|---|---|---|---|
| dictionary | abrupt | predict | import | locally |
| verdict | locate | portable | transport | bankrupt |
| dictate | location | erupt | passport | export |
| contradict | rupture | interrupt | disrupt | dislocate |

**Words in Context** Write a list word to complete each sentence.

1. Please turn off your cell phone so it doesn't ____ the movie.

2. Scientists say the volcano will ____ any day now.

3. The explosion was caused by a ____ in the gas line.

4. His ____ departure surprised everyone.

5. It is not polite to ____ when someone is speaking.

6. The company lost all its customers and went ____.

7. We ____ tractors to Thailand.

8. We ____ toys from China.

9. The girls bought a ____ stove for their camping trip.

10. The jumbo jet will ____ us across the ocean.

11. You must have a ____ to visit a foreign country.

12. Jason might ____ his shoulder if he lifts the heavy crate.

13. Fresh fruits and vegetables were sold ____.

14. The manager hopes moving to a new ____ will improve business.

15. Were you able to ____ your missing shoe?

1. _____

2. _____

3. _____

4. _____

5. _____

6. _____

7. _____

8. _____

9. _____

10. _____

11. _____

12. _____

13. _____

14. _____

15. _____

**Definitions** Write the list word that matches each definition.

16. a book that tells how to say words

17. to make a statement of disagreement

18. a jury's statement of guilt or innocence

19. to speak words aloud for someone to write down

20. to say what will happen in the future

16. _____

17. _____

18. _____

19. _____

20. _____

**Home Activity** Your child wrote words with Latin roots. Use the list words in sentences and have your child spell the words.

# Latin Roots

**Proofread a Sign** The sign at the airport terminal has some errors. Circle six misspelled words and write them correctly on the lines. Find the sentence with a punctuation error and write it correctly.

**Spelling Words**

dictionary
abrupt
predict
import
locally
verdict
locate
portable
transport
bankrupt

dictate
location
erupt
passport
export
contradict
rupture
interrupt
disrupt
dislocate

Transworld Transport

Departing Passengers:

Up on arrival please have your pass port and ticket ready.

Airline rules ditate that all heavy luggage must be checked.

Keep carry-on and portible luggage with you at all times.

Locat your gate immediately.

Stay in the proper location until your flight is called

Do not desrupt other passengers with loud cell phone conversations or loud music.

1. _____   2. _____

3. _____   4. _____

5. _____   6. _____

7. _____

   _____

**Proofread Words** Circle the word that is spelled correctly. Write it.

8. The jury's _____ was not guilty.          8. _____
   verdik          verdict

9. The new evidence seemed to _____ the accepted theory.   9. _____
   contradict          contridict

10. Businesses that do not keep up with the times are likely   10. _____
    to go _____.
    bankrup          bankrupt

**School + Home** **Home Activity** Your child identified misspelled list words. Have your child dictate list words as you spell them. Make some mistakes and have your child correct your misspellings.

Name _____

# Related Words

**Words in Context** Write two related list words to complete each sentence.

Spelling Words

please
pleasant
breath
breathe
image
imagine
product
production
heal
health

triple
triplet
relate
relative
meter
metric
compose
composition
crumb
crumble

It would **(1)**____ me greatly if you were nicer
and more **(2)**____ to our neighbors.

1. _____    2. _____

My friend says being a **(3)**____ means she and her two
look-alike sisters have **(4)**____ the fun.

3. _____    4. _____

The company rushed to get the new **(5)**____ into **(6)**____ in
time for holiday sales.

5. _____    6. _____

Don't **(7)**____ on me with your bad **(8)**____!

7. _____    8. _____

A **(9)**____ is a basic unit of length in the **(10)**____ system.

9. _____    10. _____

The wound will **(11)**____, and then you will be the picture of
perfect **(12)**____.

11. _____    12. _____

At family gatherings, there's always at least one **(13)**____
who likes to **(14)**____ old family stories.

13. _____    14. _____

Mozart had the ability to **(15)**____ a lengthy musical
**(16)**____ in a short time.

15. _____    16. _____

Can you **(17)**____ what it would be like to be the exact
**(18)**____ of a famous person?

17. _____    18. _____

Even though the cake began to **(19)**____ when I picked it up,
I managed to eat every last **(20)**____.

19. _____    20. _____

**Home Activity** Your child wrote related words to complete sentences. Name a list word and ask your child to say and spell the related word.

© Pearson Education, Inc., 4

# Related Words

**Proofread a Story** Help Maggie edit her story about a family member. Circle six misspelled words and the capitalization error. Write them correctly.

---

### a family tale

I have a very pleasent and interesting elderly relative. He is ninety-five years old and is the imige of health. One of his daily health habits is to breath very deeply each morning. Then he starts exercising. Can you imagine someone who's ninety-five doing jumping jacks? I've even seen my relative do this in tripel time. Yesterday he went out and cought a fish that weighed 1,000 pounds. He reeled it in and ate the whole thing for breakfast. Maybe by now you've guessed that this compusition is a tall tale!

---

Spelling Words

please
pleasant
breath
breathe
image
imagine
product
production
heal
health

triple
triplet
relate
relative
meter
metric
compose
composition
crumb
crumble

1. _____    2. _____

3. _____    4. _____

5. _____    6. _____

7. _____

**Frequently Misspelled Words**

caught
bought

**Proofread Words** Circle the word that is spelled correctly. Write it.

| | | | | |
|---|---|---|---|---|
| 8. breth | breath | breate | **8.** | _____ |
| 9. health | helth | heathe | **9.** | _____ |
| 10. tiplet | tripplet | triplet | **10.** | _____ |
| 11. crumle | crumble | crumbel | **11.** | _____ |
| 12. metric | metrik | metic | **12.** | _____ |

**Home Activity** Your child identified misspelled list words. Make up sentences for some of the list words. Say the sentence, omitting the list word, and have your child write the missing word.

# Multisyllabic Words

## Spelling Words

| | | | | |
|---|---|---|---|---|
| reaction | prerecorded | incorrectly | incredibly | disobedient |
| disagreeable | refreshment | unbreakable | declaration | retirement |
| misdialed | undefined | unhappily | watchfully | gleefully |
| sportsmanship | repayment | questionable | displacement | midshipman |

**Word Sort** Sort the list words by their number of syllables. Write every word.

### Three-Syllable Words

1. _____
2. _____
3. _____
4. _____
5. _____
6. _____
7. _____
8. _____
9. _____
10. _____
11. _____

### Four-Syllable Words

12. _____
13. _____
14. _____
15. _____
16. _____
17. _____
18. _____

### Five-Syllable Words

19. _____
20. _____

**Home Activity** Your child learned multisyllabic words. Say each word clearly. Have your child move a penny into a box for each syllable he or she hears.

# Words with Double Consonants

| Spelling Words | | | | |
|---|---|---|---|---|
| tomorrow | borrow | different | rabbit | matter |
| written | bottle | ridden | odd | bubble |
| offer | suffer | slippers | grasshopper | worry |
| current | lettuce | saddle | shudder | hobby |

**Word Groups** Write the list word that best completes each word group.

1. One who is sick or hurt may do this.
2. This is to take on loan.
3. These will comfortably replace your shoes.
4. Everything on Earth is made of this.
5. Most salads are made of this.
6. This is something you do to pass the time.
7. When you wash the dishes, you might make this.
8. The day after today is this.
9. Something strange or awkward may also be this.
10. One who has pedaled a bicycle has done this.

1. _____
2. _____
3. _____
4. _____
5. _____
6. _____
7. _____
8. _____
9. _____
10. _____

**Analogies** Write the list word that best completes the comparison.

11. Smile is to relax as mope is to _____.
12. Road is to roadrunner as grass is to _____.
13. Kitty is to cat as bunny is to _____.
14. Tremor is to tremble as shake is to _____.
15. Light is to dark as same is to _____.
16. Seat is to bike as _____ is to horse.
17. Cereal is to box as milk is to _____.
18. Old is to past as new is to _____.
19. Type is to typed as wrote is to _____.
20. Want is to borrow as give is to _____.

11. _____
12. _____
13. _____
14. _____
15. _____
16. _____
17. _____
18. _____
19. _____
20. _____

© Pearson Education, Inc., 4

**School + Home**

**Home Activity** Your child learned words with double consonants. Use each list word in a sentence and have your child spell the word aloud.

Name _____

# Greek Word Parts

**Spelling Words**

| telephone | biography | telescope | photograph | microwave |
| diameter | barometer | microscope | headphones | microphone |
| autograph | microchip | telegraph | perimeter | paragraph |
| phonics | symphony | saxophone | periscope | megaphone |

**What You Hear** For each definition, write a list word containing *phon*.

1. a large orchestra
2. a device for sending sound by electricity
3. a funnel-shaped tube that magnifies the voice
4. a device that strengthens and broadcasts sound waves
5. a listening device fitted to the head
6. a curving musical instrument with a reed mouthpiece
7. use of sounds in words to teach beginning reading

1. _____
2. _____
3. _____
4. _____
5. _____
6. _____
7. _____

**Proofread Sentences** Circle the misspelled list word in each sentence. Write the word correctly on the line.

8. A baremoter measures air pressure.
9. I would like to get your autagraf.
10. I had to replace a computer mikrochep.
11. The perimmeter is the distance around a shape.
12. This circle has a daimeter of 3 inches.
13. Heat a cup of water in the microwav.
14. A parascope gives a submarine a view.

8. _____
9. _____
10. _____
11. _____
12. _____
13. _____
14. _____

**Greek Pairs** Use two list words with the same root to finish each sentence.

A good _____ of the subject helps you picture the subject of a _____. (*graph*)

15. _____          16. _____

You can use a _____ to see stars and a _____ to see cells (*scope*)

17. _____          18. _____

A complete _____ is a long _____ to send. (*graph*)

19. _____          20. _____

**Home Activity** Your child learned words formed from Greek word parts. Have your child look at words with *phon* and *graph*, and then tell what *phon* and *graph* probably mean.

© Pearson Education, Inc., 4

73

Name _____

# Latin Roots

```
┌─────────────────────────────────────────────────────────┐
│                    Spelling Words                        │
├─────────────────────────────────────────────────────────┤
│  dictionary   abrupt     predict      import     locally │
│  verdict      locate     portable     transport  bankrupt│
│  dictate      location   erupt        passport   export  │
│  contradict   rupture    interrupt    disrupt    dislocate│
└─────────────────────────────────────────────────────────┘
```

**Analogies** Write the list word that best completes the sentence.

1. Thesaurus is to describe as _____ is to define.
2. Judge is to award as jury is to _____.
3. License is to drive as _____ is to travel.
4. Cloud is to storm as volcano is to _____.
5. Wealth is to rich as poverty is to _____.
6. Like is to dislike as lose is to _____.

1. _____
2. _____
3. _____
4. _____
5. _____
6. _____

**Paragraph Completion** Use list words with *port* to complete the paragraph.

Trains, ships, trucks, and airplanes **7.** _____ goods all over the world. Years ago, most materials were less **8.** _____ than they are now. The age of machines allows countries to **9.** _____ goods they have to sell and to **10.** _____ goods they need.

7. _____          8. _____
9. _____         10. _____

**Word Scramble** Unscramble the letters and write the list word.

11. pratub       _____
12. pertcid      _____
13. lalcoly      _____
14. icedatt      _____
15. notacoil     _____
16. ratnodticc   _____
17. puretur      _____
18. pinetrrut    _____
19. trupsid      _____
20. etadiscol    _____

**Home Activity** Your child learned words formed from Latin roots. Help your child brainstorm a list of additional words with *dic*, *rupt*, *port*, and *loc*.

© Pearson Education, Inc., 4

74

Name _____

# Related Words

**Adding Word Endings** Base words may change when a word ending is added. Write the pairs of list words in the correct column.

**Drop *e*,
Add Word Ending**

1. _____

2. _____

3. _____

4. _____

**No Change,
Add Word Ending**

5. _____

6. _____

7. _____

8. _____

9. _____

**Change Base Word
Add Word Ending**

10. _____

**Home Activity** Your child has learned pairs of related words. Challenge your child to use each pair of words in a sentence. Listen for correct pronunciation.

Name _____

# Schwa

**Spelling Words**

| | | | | |
|---|---|---|---|---|
| stomach | memory | Canada | element | mystery |
| science | remember | forget | suppose | iron |
| gravel | difficult | fortune | giant | architect |
| normal | notify | privilege | cement | yesterday |

**Antonyms** Write the list word that has the opposite or almost the opposite meaning.

**1.** tomorrow _____     **2.** easy _____

**3.** remember _____     **4.** miniature _____

**5.** strange _____     **6.** forget _____

**Synonyms** Write a list word that has the same or almost the same meaning.

**7.** tummy _____     **8.** suspense _____

**9.** luck _____     **10.** designer _____

**11.** advantage _____     **12.** remembrance _____

**Missing Words** Complete the sentence by writing a list word.

**13.** I _____ she will arrive on time.     **13.** _____

**14.** The new _____ sidewalk has no cracks.     **14.** _____

**15.** Walking barefoot on _____ is painful.     **15.** _____

**16.** Please _____ me when my package arrives.     **16.** _____

**17.** Montreal is a city in Quebec, _____.     **17.** _____

**18.** She is determined that people say she has a will of _____.     **18.** _____

**19.** His _____ experiment took 30 minutes.     **19.** _____

**20.** The _____ of surprise is important to a good story.     **20.** _____

**Home Activity** Your child wrote words that have the schwa sound. Say the list words and have your child spell them.

# Schwa

**Proofread a Report** Circle six misspelled words in Alex's report. Write the words correctly. Find the sentence with capitalization errors and write it correctly.

Northern Lights

The shimmering show of the Northern Lights used to be a mystary, but thanks to sciunce we now know the cause. Like iron to a magnet, particles in the sky are attracted to the Earth.

The amazing sky show is best seen in places like Canida or Alaska, but it is diffacult to predict when a show will happen. Nature does not Notify Us in Advance. There is always an element of surprise. However, it is norml to see Northern Lights in August.

Seeing a Northern Light show creates a beutaful memory. If you have the good fortune to see the wonderful sight, you will never forget it.

1. _____     2. _____

3. _____     4. _____

5. _____     6. _____

7. _____

**Proofread Words** Cross out the misspelled list word in each phrase. Write the word correctly.

8. archatect designs a plan          8. _____

9. strong ciment sidewalks           9. _____

10. designs for ginat homes          10. _____

11. beautiful gravle walkways        11. _____

12. plans completed yesturday        12. _____

**Home Activity** Your child identified misspelled list words. Say each word in a sentence and have your child repeat the list word and write it.

Name _____

# Prefixes *mis-*, *non-*, *re-*, *pre-*

**Missing Words** Write the list word that best completes each sentence.

1. Textbooks and biographies are examples of ____ books.

2. To avoid standing in line, we ____ for our movie tickets.

3. My friends from kindergarten and I got together for a ____.

4. My suitcase was too full to close so I had to ____ it.

5. The forward got the ____ and made a basket.

6. The trip from Atlanta to Seattle was a direct, ____ flight.

7. The eye doctor had to ____ my glasses because they didn't fit.

8. We ____ much of our food to save time.

9. It is hard to make friends if you ____ people.

10. A ____ pan is easy to clean.

11. When boating, you should wear a life preserver as a ____.

12. There was a ____ in last week's magazine.

1. _____
2. _____
3. _____
4. _____
5. _____
6. _____
7. _____
8. _____
9. _____
10. _____
11. _____
12. _____

**Antonyms** Write the list word that has the opposite meaning.

13. find

14. luck

15. truth

16. add

17. relapse

18. reopen

19. obedience

20. money-making

13. _____
14. _____
15. _____
16. _____
17. _____
18. _____
19. _____
20. _____

© Pearson Education, Inc., 4

**Home Activity** Your child wrote words with the prefixes *mis-*, *non-*, *re-* and *pre-*. Ask your child to explain how each prefix changes the base word's meaning.

Name _____

# Prefixes *mis-*, *non-*, *re-*, *pre-*

**Proofread Rules** All the rules, except the last rule, give bad advice and should not be followed! Circle six words that are misspelled. Write the words correctly. Write the sentence that has an incorrect pronoun correctly.

Misplace your homework so you can't find it.

Always prejuge people so they'll be mad at you.

Talk non stop about something boring for hours.

Open envelopes and then resel it.

Tell everyone that you're having a reunion and don't go.

Reajust the volume on the radio to wake everyone up.

Beleve everything you see on television.

Make sure you know that everything on this list is nosense.

1. _____     2. _____

3. _____     4. _____

5. _____     6. _____

7. _____

**Proofread Words** Circle the correct spelling. Write the correct word.

| | | | |
|---|---|---|---|
| **8.** non profit | non-profet | nonprofit | **8.** _____ |
| **9.** precook | pre-cook | pre cook | **9.** _____ |
| **10.** misfortuun | misfortune | misfortoon | **10.** _____ |
| **11.** rekover | recovar | recover | **11.** _____ |
| **12.** precaution | pre caution | precation | **12.** _____ |

**Home Activity** Your child identified misspelled words with the prefixes *mis-*, *non-*, *re-*, and *pre-*. Say the base words of some of the list words. Have your child add the prefix and spell the list word.

Name _____

# Suffixes *-less*, *-ment*, *-ness*

**Synonyms** Write the list word that has the same or nearly the same meaning.

1. roadway    1. _____
2. eternal    2. _____
3. kindness    3. _____
4. fidgety    4. _____
5. penalty    5. _____
6. gasping    6. _____
7. declaration    7. _____
8. pleasure    8. _____

**Antonyms** Write the list word that has the opposite or nearly the opposite meaning.

9. few    9. _____
10. injustice    10. _____
11. hopeful    11. _____
12. unimportance    12. _____
13. lazy    13. _____
14. imperfect    14. _____
15. essential    15. _____

**Missing Words** Complete the sentence by writing a list word.

16. Rest is one ___ for the flu.    16. _____
17. We went to an ___ park.    17. _____
18. Don't forget to make the monthly ___.    18. _____
19. The child looked at the magician with ___.    19. _____
20. The doctor said the exam would be ___.    20. _____

© Pearson Education, Inc., 4

**Home Activity** Your child wrote words with the suffixes *-less*, *-ment*, and *-ness*. Say a base word and have your child add a suffix to spell the list word.

# Suffixes *-less*, *-ment*, *-ness*

**Proofread an Essay** Help Jake corect his essay for the school writing contest. Circle six misspelled words and one capitalization error. Write the words correctly.

| | |
|---|---|
| **Spelling Words** | |
| countless | |
| payment | |
| goodness | |
| fairness | |
| hopeless | |
| treatment | |
| statement | |
| breathless | |
| restless | |
| enjoyment | |
| | |
| pavement | |
| flawless | |
| tireless | |
| amazement | |
| amusement | |
| greatness | |
| punishment | |
| timeless | |
| needless | |
| painless | |

### The Key to Success

How does one reach grateness? Does it take countless hours of tireles work? Does it mean sticking with something even when things look hopless? Does it mean pounding the paivment trying to convince others that you have a great idea? To be successful, you must do all these things, but you must also find enjoiment in your work. After all, the best payment is a job well done. Thomas a. Edison knew this. It tok over 10,000 experiments to invent the light bulb.

1. _____  2. _____

3. _____  4. _____

5. _____  6. _____

7. _____

**Proofread Words** Cross out the list words that are spelled incorrectly. Write the words correctly.

8. After running the 100-meter race, the runners were breatheless.

8. _____

9. No one liked the commissioner's statment about the new baseball rule.

9. _____

10. Pets must rely on the goddness of their owners.

10. _____

11. Celebrities always get special treatement at restaurants.

11. _____

12. Waiting always makes me resless.

12. _____

**Frequently Misspelled Words**

took
myself

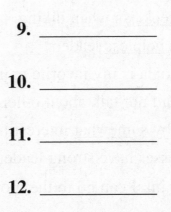

**Home Activity** Your child identified misspelled words with the suffixes *-less*, *-ment*, and *-ness*. Say one of the suffixes and have your child find and spell all the list words that end with that suffix.

Name _____

# Suffixes *-ful*, *-ly*, *-ion*

**Rhymes** Complete each sentence with a list word that rhymes with the underlined word.

1. When you have <u>only</u> one friend, sometimes you'll be ____.     1. _____

2. Recycling is one <u>solution</u> to the problem of ____.     2. _____

3. He spends other people's money ____ but his own <u>meagerly</u>.     3. _____

4. Reporters write <u>factually</u> but ____ make mistakes.     4. _____

5. I love my great aunt <u>dearly</u>, but I only see her ____.     5. _____

6. If you can handle times that are <u>stressful</u>, you will be ____.     6. _____

7. Toys by the <u>trayful</u> can make you feel ____.     7. _____

8. To my <u>recollection</u>, my homework required no ____.     8. _____

9. Our new puppy ____ started to behave <u>decently</u>.     9. _____

10. Thorns by the <u>armful</u> are bound to be ____.     10. _____

11. He asked me a <u>question</u> so I made a ____.     11. _____

12. Did you buy something ____, or were you just <u>wasteful</u>?     12. _____

**Antonyms** Write the list word that has the opposite meaning of the underlined word.

13. That was very <u>inconsiderate</u> of you.     13. _____

14. You must be <u>reckless</u> when hiking.     14. _____

15. Presidents are <u>helpless</u> leaders.     15. _____

16. The <u>warlike</u> koala is my favorite animal.     16. _____

17. He <u>foolishly</u> did not talk about others.     17. _____

18. I find my hobby <u>somewhat</u> interesting.     18. _____

19. <u>Failing</u> businesses have strong leadership.     19. _____

20. I <u>doubtfully</u> think I can go to the movies.     20. _____

© Pearson Education, Inc., 4

**Home Activity** Your child wrote words with suffixes *-ful*, *-ly*, and *-ion*. Take turns writing and saying the list words.

82

Name _____

# Suffixes *-ful*, *-ly*, *-ion*

**Proofread an Article** This short article needs to be corrected before it goes to the printer. Circle six misspelled words. Write the words correctly. Write the word with a capitalization error correctly.

---

A Healthy Vacation

Have you ever considered going to a spa? Spas are especally common in europe. Spas are actually places to go to get healthier. People who go to them are extremly motivated to improve their health. Visitors begin by meeting with an expert for an exercise or diet suggestion. The experts wisly ask questions before making recommendations. The atmosphere in a spa is peacefull. The decorations are tastful. People learn to use their powerful self-discipline for exercise and diet. If the visit is succesful, they go home rested and relaxed and with the tools they need for a healthy, new lifestyle.

---

1. _____      2. _____

3. _____      4. _____

5. _____      6. _____

7. _____

© Pearson Education, Inc., 4

**Proofread Words** Circle the correct spelling. Write the correct list word on the line.

| 8. | egerly | eagerly | egerally | 8. _____ |
| 9. | suggestion | sugestion | suggesjun | 9. _____ |
| 10. | yerly | yearly | yearally | 10. _____ |
| 11. | sertinly | certinally | certainly | 11. _____ |
| 12. | playfull | playful | plaful | 12. _____ |

**Home Activity** Your child identified misspelled words with the suffixes *-ful*, *-ly*, and *-ion*. Let your child dictate words for you to spell. Make some mistakes and let your child correct them.

# Silent Consonants

| Spelling Words | | | | |
|---|---|---|---|---|
| island | column | knee | often | known |
| castle | thumb | half | wring | whistle |
| autumn | knuckles | numb | Illinois | rhyme |
| climber | limb | plumbing | unwritten | clothes |

**Missing Words** Write a list word to complete each familiar saying.

1. "To go out on a ____" means to take a chance.　　1. _____

2. "A rule of ____" is something that is generally true.　　2. _____

3. To "wet your ____" means to take a drink.　　3. _____

4. "A ____ jerk reaction" is a gut reaction or feeling.　　4. _____

5. "There's no ____ or reason" means it doesn't make sense.　　5. _____

6. If your "glass is ____ full" you always look on the bright side.　　6. _____

**Complete** Write a list word to complete each sentence.

7. The author's book is still ____.　　7. _____

8. We built a sand ____ at the beach.　　8. _____

9. I like to buy new ____.　　9. _____

10. Abraham Lincoln spent much of his life in Springfield, ____.　　10. _____

11. George Washington was ____ as a person who didn't lie.　　11. _____

12. Something you do all the time is an activity you do ____.　　12. _____

13. Without gloves, my fingers became ____ from the cold.　　13. _____

14. Apple harvests and colorful leaves are the nice things about ____.　　14. _____

15. Your ____ are the joints in your fingers.　　15. _____

16. Dip the sponge in water and ____ it dry.　　16. _____

17. When the pipes squeak, it may be time to get some new ____.　　17. _____

18. Hawaii is an ____ state.　　18. _____

19. The mountain ____ is very skilled.　　19. _____

20. The teacher wrote a long ____ of numbers for us to add.　　20. _____

**Home Activity** Your child wrote words that have silent consonants. Pronounce each list word incorrectly, saying the silent consonant as in *iz-land*. Have your child correct your pronunciation and spell the word.

© Pearson Education, Inc., 4

# Silent Consonants

**Proofread a Poster** As a joke, Jack's pals made up this poster. Circle seven words that are spelled incorrectly. Write the words correctly. Circle a verb that does not agree with its subject, and write the correct form of the verb.

Have you seen Illinoi Jack?

His sleeves covers his nuckles, and he always has some chocolate in his pocket.

His cloths are full of patches, and he is as pale as a gost.

Jack is known for his ability to rhyme and whisle.

He will fix your plumming when he is not writing poems.

Jack is offen seen with his pet calf, Nellie.

| | |
|---|---|
| 1. _____ | 2. _____ |
| 3. _____ | 4. _____ |
| 5. _____ | 6. _____ |
| 7. _____ | 8. _____ |

**Complete the Word** Each word below has a missing letter. Write the complete word on the line.

9. autum _____   10. iland _____

11. haf _____   12. casle _____

13. colum _____   14. num _____

15. thum _____   16. lim _____

17. climer _____   18. nee _____

19. nown _____   20. Chrismas _____

**Spelling Words**

island
column
knee
often
known
castle
thumb
half
wring
whistle

autumn
knuckles
numb
Illinois
rhyme
climber
limb
plumbing
unwritten
clothes

**Frequently Misspelled Words**

Christmas
chocolate
would

**Home Activity** Your child identified misspelled words with silent consonants. Have your child find three words with silent *k* and make up a rule about when *k* is silent.

# Schwa

| Spelling Words | | | | |
| --- | --- | --- | --- | --- |
| stomach | memory | Canada | element | mystery |
| science | remember | forget | suppose | iron |
| gravel | difficult | fortune | giant | architect |
| normal | notify | privilege | cement | yesterday |

**Words in Context** Write a list word to complete each sentence.

1. Voting is an American's basic _____.

2. Grandpa's _____ of World War II is clear.

3. The _____ of this building did a great job.

4. What happened to the Roanoke colony is a _____.

5. It is difficult to walk on a _____ road barefoot.

6. The post office will _____ you when the package comes.

7. She made a _____ by starting an Internet company.

8. My _____ pumpkin won first prize at the county fair.

9. It is warmer today than it was _____.

10. _____ lies on the northern border of the United States.

1. _____

2. _____

3. _____

4. _____

5. _____

6. _____

7. _____

8. _____

9. _____

10. _____

**Word Meanings** Write the list word beside its definition.

11. pouch in digestive system for receiving food

12. a substance made up of atoms that are alike

13. to bring back to mind

14. to imagine, think, or guess

15. a metallic element used to make steel

16. to fail to remember

17. hard to do or understand

18. a substance used to make concrete

19. average; agreeing with the usual standard

20. knowledge gained by observation and experiment

11. _____

12. _____

13. _____

14. _____

15. _____

16. _____

17. _____

18. _____

19. _____

20. _____

**Home Activity** Your child learned words that contain the schwa sound. Write each word, leaving a blank for the letter with the schwa sound. Have your child complete each word.

Name _____

# Prefixes *mis-, non-, re-, pre-*

| Spelling Words | | | | |
|---|---|---|---|---|
| misplace | nonsense | prepay | repack | misfortune |
| remove | precook | nonstop | recover | reseal |
| misbehavior | reunion | nonfiction | rebound | prejudge |
| readjust | misprint | nonprofit | nonstick | precaution |

**Word Meanings** Write the list word beside its meaning.

1. bad luck                                          1. _____
2. to arrange again to make fit                      2. _____
3. gathering of people who have been apart           3. _____
4. silliness; gibberish                              4. _____
5. bad conduct                                       5. _____
6. to take away                                      6. _____
7. to prepare food in advance                        7. _____
8. to bounce back                                    8. _____
9. to judge too early                                9. _____
10. to get back after losing                         10. _____

**Analogies** Write the list word that best completes the sentence.

11. Praise is to criticize as find is to _____.       11. _____
12. Haiku is to poetry as biography is to _____.      12. _____
13. View is to preview as pay is to _____.            13. _____
14. Plan is to preplan as caution is to _____.        14. _____
15. Jet is to airplane as direct is to _____.         15. _____
16. Corporate is to profit as volunteer is to _____.  16. _____
17. Fact checker is to error as proofreader is to _____. 17. _____
18. Pavement is to road as _____ is to pots and pans. 18. _____
19. Open is to close as unwrap is to _____.           19. _____
20. Load is to unload as unpack is to _____.          20. _____

© Pearson Education, Inc., 4

**Home Activity** Your child learned words with the prefixes *mis-, non-, re-* and *pre-*. Write each list word without its prefix. Write the prefixes in bold on sticky notes. Have your child add prefixes to spell each list word.

87

Name _____

# Suffixes *-less*, *-ment*, *-ness*

| Spelling Words | | | | |
|---|---|---|---|---|
| countless | payment | goodness | fairness | hopeless |
| treatment | statement | breathless | restless | enjoyment |
| pavement | flawless | tireless | amazement | amusement |
| greatness | punishment | timeless | needless | painless |

**Word Search** Circle the list words in the puzzle.

```
P A Y M E N T Y B T W P C
G A M A Z E M E N T F S O
O E O E I U A E B E A S U
O S T A T E M E N T I E N
D I A B C H U X Z E R N T
N K L B S X S J M H N T L
E C A I O R E R D O E A E
S R N F V P M A L P S E S
S U R H O P E L E S S R S
P B W E D Q N T C L H G H
H A K R V R T C A E L E N
```

payment
statement
goodness
punishment
countless
amazement
amusement
hopeless
fairness
greatness

**Words in Context** Write a list word to complete each sentence.

1. The dress has a _____ quality. It won't go out of style.
2. The workers put new _____ on the road.
3. Running the long race made me tired and _____.
4. I love good books and often read for _____.
5. The doctor prescribed a _____ for my ear infection.
6. Teeth cleaning is _____. It doesn't hurt at all!
7. The firefighters were _____. They did not rest.
8. I was _____ and could barely sleep. I was too excited!
9. The perfect diamond in Lucy's wedding ring was _____.
10. It's _____ to wash the floor again. Dad did it yesterday.

1. _____
2. _____
3. _____
4. _____
5. _____
6. _____
7. _____
8. _____
9. _____
10. _____

© Pearson Education, Inc., 4

**School + Home** **Home Activity** Your child learned words with the suffixes *-less*, *-ment*, and *-ness*. Read a magazine article with your child and locate more words with these suffixes.

Name _____

# Suffixes *-ful*, *-ly*, *-ion*

| Spelling Words | | | | |
|---|---|---|---|---|
| careful | tasteful | lonely | powerful | suggestion |
| peaceful | recently | extremely | certainly | wisely |
| harmful | monthly | yearly | successful | playful |
| thoughtful | actually | pollution | correction | eagerly |

**Synonyms** Write the list word that has the same, or nearly the same, meaning as the word.

1. cautious _____
2. calm _____
3. light-hearted _____
4. strong _____
5. damaging _____
6. deserted _____
7. sensibly _____
8. really _____

**Words in Context** Write a list word from the box to complete each sentence.

9. We waited _____ for summer vacation to begin.
10. A _____ person considers the feelings of others.
11. A _____ note to the winner shows good sportsmanship.
12. I have a _____ for how to improve crowding in schools.
13. Most families pay their bills _____.
14. Prices have gone up a lot _____.
15. Mom was _____ angry when we lied about our grades.
16. An egg dropped seven stories will _____ break.
17. If you ask politely, you are more likely to be _____.
18. The Nobel Prizes are awarded _____ in the fall.
19. _____ poisons our air and water.
20. The teacher pointed out a _____ that was needed.

9. _____
10. _____
11. _____
12. _____
13. _____
14. _____
15. _____
16. _____
17. _____
18. _____
19. _____
20. _____

**Home Activity** Your child learned words with the suffixes *-ful*, *-ly*, and *-ion*. Have your child pick ten list words. Together write a story about your family using the words.

# Silent Consonants

**Classifying** Write the list word that fits each group.

1. princess, knight, dragon, _____
2. hip, ankle, wrist, _____
3. Ohio, Iowa, Nebraska, _____
4. twist, squeeze, mangle, _____
5. winter, spring, summer, _____
6. pinky, toe, index, _____
7. sing, hum, warble, _____
8. trunk, roots, leaves, _____
9. rhythm, metaphor, alliteration, _____
10. coats, blouses, pants, _____

1. _____
2. _____
3. _____
4. _____
5. _____
6. _____
7. _____
8. _____
9. _____
10. _____

**Word Scramble** Unscramble the list words and write the letters on the lines.

11. dinlas _____
12. monclu _____
13. fonet _____
14. wonnk _____
15. flah _____

16. snukklec _____
17. bmnu _____
18. crimelb _____
19. blingmup _____
20. twinnerut _____

**School + Home** **Home Activity** Your child learned words with silent consonants. Say each word and have your child name its silent letter.